Roland Stühmer

Web-oriented Event Processing

Web-oriented Event Processing

by
Roland Stühmer

KIT Scientific Publishing

Genehmigte Dissertation, Karlsruher Institut für Technologie (KIT)
Fakultät für Wirtschaftswissenschaften, 2014
Tag der mündlichen Prüfung: 17. Juli 2014
Referent: Prof. Dr. Rudi Studer
Korreferent: Prof. Dr. Opher Etzion

Impressum

KIT Scientific Publishing

Karlsruher Institut für Technologie (KIT)
KIT Scientific Publishing
Straße am Forum 2
D-76131 Karlsruhe

KIT Scientific Publishing is a registered trademark of Karlsruhe Institute of Technology. Reprint using the book cover is not allowed.

www.ksp.kit.edu

Print on Demand 2014

ISBN 978-3-7315-0265-4
DOI 10.5445/KSP/1000043122

Abstract

Event processing – computing performed on occurrences happening in a system or domain – is a common methodology of dealing with real-time data where situations must be detected instantaneously. Event processing research and products today provide a good understanding and support for closed-domain systems such as enterprises. On the Web real-time results also gain interest as more and more data are available in data streams. Examples are social activity streams or sensor readings. Requirements for event processing on the Web are, however, different from those in closed-domain systems. The question then arises as to how the Web can be made situation-aware. In this thesis we collect the requirements for a Real-time Web and answer the posed question by contributing the design and realisation of a Web-oriented event processing system to manage events, streams and queries.

The presented result is a semantic system that serves as an Event Marketplace: heterogeneous events from the Web modelled in RDF are matched and integrated using a processing language we designed and describe in this work. The system consists of these main components: an event processing layer to combine, integrate, filter and derive events quickly, in memory, and a storage layer to maintain historic events augmenting the real-time layer with long-term queries. Event-driven applications are implemented on this architecture by expressions in our language supporting hybrid queries combining both real-time queries (on pushed data) and historic queries (on pull data). A governance component enforces efficient access control on event streams and storage. The main contributions of the system design are its Web-orientation by adhering to open and extensible standards, its processing language offering the combination of real-time and historical queries on events and its governance capabilities creating a multitenant system based on permissions. The system uses Web technologies such as Linked Data, RDF and SPARQL to model, organise, locate, process and control access to events.

We evaluate the artefacts produced as part of this work using qualitative and quantitative measures: Qualitative comparisons are made with the State of the Art and the overall cost of our Web-based approach is determined quantitatively and compared to a non-Web-based solution as the baseline.

I have received a great deal of encouragement

I am deeply thankful to Prof. Dr. **Rudi Studer** for creating a creative and productive environment in Semantic Web research. He leads people by example and he makes it a delight to be in his team and to prove oneself. Prof. Dr. **Opher Etzion** is the author of one of the most important books on event processing and I am proud to have him on my jury. I appreciate his calmness and his independent thinking regarding technologies and their hypes. Moreover I am thankful to Prof. Dr. **Thomas Setzer** and Prof. Dr. **Jan Kowalski** for participating in the jury and thinking the thoughts of different research fields with appreciation.

I would like to thank my mentor **Nenad Stojanovic** for supporting my ideas, managing the research group very effectively, always pushing for more creativity, and sharing his excitement for Web technologies. Nonetheless, I would like to thank **Ljiljana Stojanovic** for her tireless scientific rigour and attention to detail which impresses me and greatly benefited my work. Their qualities make Ljiljana and Nenad the rare and admirable team that they are.

I have enjoyed many entertaining and fruitful discussions with my friends and co-workers: Special thanks go to **Dominik Riemer** for supporting me in situations of doubt, to **Jürgen Bock** for being a steady advocate since I started my work, **Benedikt Kämpgen** for his spontaneous help, sharp eyes and questions screening my work, to **Valentin Zacharias** for his motivating inquisitiveness and unorthodox thinking and finally to **Darko Aničić** for his foundational work. Extra special thanks go to **Heike Döhmer** whose omnipresence paired with cheerful attitude assured me that any problem can be overcome and that the workplace should be a happy place.

I am thankful to **Stefan Obermeier** for helping me implement the system with great technical detail and for enduring my expectations for diligence. I am also thankful to **Ningyuan Pan** for helping with the implementation and for his effort in starting the future directions of this work.

I would like to gratefully mention the **European Union** whose research grants SYNERGY and PLAY enabled me to conduct my work. The grants allowed me to work in challenging, international environments. Some of the many interesting persons I met deserve special thanks: **Yiannis Verginadis** for his compassionate diplomacy and his help in critical phases of work, **Iyad Alshabani** for finding pragmatic and effective solutions during our international collaboration, **Laurent Pellegrino** for setting good examples of software quality, **Christophe Hamerling** for teaching me the tools of software engineering, Prof. Dr. **Françoise Baude**, Prof. Dr. **Frédérick Bénaben** and **Philippe Gibert** for their fruitful collaboration and the warm welcome and finally **Aleksandar Stojadinović** for transferring some of my results in a production setting.

I wish to thank my parents **Elisabeth and Gerhard Stühmer** who had enabled me to study Informatics. Long before that they instilled in me a love of science and language, all of which finds a place in this thesis. I am thankful for my younger brother and only sibling **Stephan Stühmer**, he has been a very good friend throughout the years. I would like to commemorate my **grandmother** for her placidness and my **great-aunt** for her impeccable manners. Both influenced me long beyond their parting. Finally, I would like to thank **Jana Eubel**. She is an inspiration and a motivation to get ahead in life and to get things done. I am happy to have met her.

Contents

Figures

Tables

Listings

Abbreviations

API	Application programming interface
BDPL	Big Data Processing Language
BNF	Backus-Naur Form
DCEP	Distributed Complex Event Processing
EDA	Event-driven architecture
ELE	ETALIS Language for Events
EP	Event processing
IoS	Internet of Services
IoT	Internet of Things
JSON	JavaScript Object Notation
LD	Linked Data
OWL	Web Ontology Language
RDF	Resource Description Framework
RDFS	Resource Description Framework Schema
REST	Representational state transfer
SDK	Software development kit

SOA	Service-oriented architecture
SOAP	Simple Object Access Protocol
SPARQL	SPARQL Protocol and RDF Query Language
SSN	Semantic Sensor Network
XML	Extensible Markup Language
XPath	XML Path Language

1 Introduction

In this thesis we are pursuing the idea of bringing event processing (EP) [Luckham 2001] to the Web. Recently, there has been a significant paradigm shift towards a Real-time Web. Previously, requests for Web sites just like queries against databases were concerned with looking at what happened in the past. On the other hand, event processing is concerned with processing real-time occurrences, i.e. event processing is concerned with events which are just happening.

An event is something that happens, or is contemplated as happening [Etzion and Niblett 2010]. For example, on the Web an event may signify a sensor reading, a price-change signal, some piece of information becoming available, a deviation and so forth. An event can also represent something that did not happen (e.g. the contemplation of absence of an event within a certain time frame).

Using event processing this thesis describes an architecture for dynamic and complex, event-driven interaction for the Web. Such an architecture will enable the exchange of real-time data (events) between heterogeneous services, providing possibilities of optimizing and personalizing the execution of services on the Web, resulting in context-driven adaptivity.

To deal with heterogeneity on the Web we propose an event format based on Resource Description Framework (RDF) [Klyne and Carroll 2004] with a matching event pattern language syntax based on SPARQL Protocol and RDF Query Language (SPARQL) [Harris and Seaborne 2010]. Both of these base-technologies are currently used on the Web as general methods for conceptual modelling (and querying, respectively) of information. We have adapted them to enable a Real-time Web based on these well-known foundations, i.e. RDF and SPARQL. Non-functional aspects such as privacy for real-time data on the Web are also addressed using these foundations.

The motivation for our work is the idea of the Web being situation-aware in real-time. This idea was developed as a grand challenge [Chandy et al. 2011] for event processing. The purpose of this challenge is "to identify a single, though broad challenge that impacts society and at the same time measures the progress of research" [Chandy et al. 2011]. The challenge is to create a decentralised, global, Internet-like infrastructure built upon widely-accepted open standards [Chandy et al. 2011]. We will discuss the requirements in detail in Chapter 2.

There are a number of terms (synonyms) given for a Web which is situation-aware. Examples are Real-time Web[1], Web of Events[2], Active Web[3], Reactive Web[4] and Event Processing Fabric[5].

They have in common that data must be exchanged quickly after it is created. Moreover, Fromm [Fromm 2009] states that the Real-time Web (i) is a new form of communication which (ii) creates a new body of content,

[1]Ken Fromm: [Fromm 2009]
[2]Ramesh Jain keynote: [Jain 2007]
[3]Krzysztof Ostrowski: [Ostrowski et al. 2007]
[4]François Bry: [Bry and Eckert 2006]
[5]Event processing manifesto: [Chandy et al. 2011]

(iii) is real-time, (iv) is public with an explicitly associated social graph and (v) carries an implicit model of federation. Indeed, this work makes a contribution to the Real-time Web by enabling a new form of communication using event processing, working in real-time and supporting federated data-creation and consumption.

There are many technological developments on the Web today which can create a lot of events and thus support a Real-time Web. Such events are delivered in a push fashion as opposed to the traditional client–server Web of request and response. For one, there is the W3C Web Notification Working Group[6] which is working on push notifications to actively notify running Web applications. Additionally, HTML5 defines two techniques to facilitate communication initiated by the server. These techniques are *Server-Sent Events*[7] and *WebSockets*[8]. They operate at different layers of the protocol stack to achieve push delivery to Web clients. Another approach to push-data on the Web is the Google *PubSubHubbub* protocol[9] to enable mainly server-to-server notifications. It is designed to avoid inefficient polling of news feeds in Atom or RSS. Lastly, the Facebook Graph API provides a large-scale example of an application-specific way to subscribe to real-time updates[10] from changes to connected people's profiles.

With event processing in itself and with Web technologies such as described in this thesis below we can get closer to reaching the goals of the grand challenge such as distributed ownership and community-based self-curation and updating of event schemas and queries.

1.1. Research Questions

The principal research question for this work is presented first. It combines research about the Web on the one hand and on real-time data on the

[6]Web Notification Working Group: http://www.w3.org/2010/06/notification-charter
[7]Server-Sent Events: http://www.w3.org/TR/eventsource/
[8]WebSocket API: http://www.w3.org/TR/websockets/
[9]Google PubSubHubbub protocol http://code.google.com/p/pubsubhubbub/
[10]Facebook Graph API Real-time Updates https://developers.facebook.com/docs/graph-api/real-time-updates

other. The question is subsequently broken down into three sub-questions which will be answered in and be the primary topic of the main chapters (5 to 7).

The principal research question is:

How can the Web be made situation-aware?

The question addresses (i) situation awareness and (ii) the Web. Situation awareness is defined in [Endsley and Garland 2000] as "the perception of the elements in the environment within a volume of time and space, the comprehension of their meaning, and the projection of their status in the near future." For this work we focus on the first part, *perception* which is about "knowing what is going on" [Endsley and Garland 2000].

The Web is the second part of the question. The Web consists of resources which can be queried for their current state by accessing these resources. Additionally, indexes such as search engines exist. They can also be used to get information about the state of resources.

To gain awareness about situations on the Web, however, timeliness is important. Therefore, it is not efficient to query (i.e. pull) all of the Web's resources regularly to capture state changes as soon as they happen (cf. Section 3.4 on the discussion of push and pull communication). Centralised indexes can only at best achieve near real-time performance (i.e. by pulling at high frequencies). Moreover, such indexes usually do not cover large portions of the Web.

Therefore, to gain situation awareness on the Web, time-critical data must be exchanged in a push fashion. The paradigm for such data processing is *event processing* which is often (but not necessarily) connected with push-data.

This thesis does not impose restrictions on the type and volume of data that are exchanged on the Real-Time Web. Specifically, no statements are being made as to what part of the data is persisted and available later and what part is discarded immediately and is only available via aggregations. Such decisions are left to be application-specific.

Event processing is used during the course of this work to answer many parts of the principal research question. Event processing consists of three ingredients: events (i.e. the data), event patterns (i.e. the logic) and event processing engines (i.e. the infrastructure). Hence, the following research questions ask about these three ingredients one by one, with special focus on their use on the Web.

Research Question 1 (Web Interoperability). *How can we achieve event interoperability for situation awareness at a Web scale?*

This research question deals with the *data* which must be exchanged on the Web to gain situation awareness. We will consider our answer to this question as going beyond the question of static data interoperability. Additions are made for specificities to situation awareness such as time and/or place of situations as defined above. The requirements to answer this question are collected in detail in Chapter 2, *Requirements*, and are resolved in Chapter 5.

Research Question 2 (Processing Language). *How to design and realise a processing language for Web events?*

The second research question deals with the *logics* of situation awareness. Specifically, this question targets a formalism to define more complex situations on the basis of simpler situations in an operational way. This sort of inductive definition is borrowed from event processing where derived events (i.e. more complex situations) are created based on simpler events (simpler situations). The target of this question is a language which formalises the derivation of events from other events. Detailed requirements for such a language are collected in our chapter on requirements and are resolved in Chapter 6.

Research Question 3 (Infrastructure). *How to design and develop an efficient infrastructure supporting a Web of events?*

This research question deals with the matter of the information system behind the approach. Infrastructure is required to evaluate the logic mentioned above. Meanwhile, the efficiency of the approach must be suitable for the application scenarios. Detailed requirements for an infrastructure supporting situation awareness on the Web are collected in our chapter on requirements and are resolved in Chapter 7.

1.2. Research Paradigm and Methodology

The aforementioned research questions are addressed in this thesis through qualitative and quantitative means using the paradigm of design science as it is known for information systems research.

Design science as described in [Hevner et al. 2004] "seeks to extend the boundaries of human and organizational capabilities by creating new and innovative artefacts".

Innovative artefacts in the sense of design science can be vocabularies, models, methods and instantiations (implemented and prototype systems). For this thesis we produced models for events (cf. Chapter 5), models and methods for queries (cf. Chapter 6) and an instantiation of a prototype system (cf. Chapter 7).

1.3. Contributions of this Thesis

This thesis contributes an implemented system for processing real-time data from events on the Web using open standards needed for adoption on the Web. The system is comprised of three main contributions. They are developed addressing the three main research questions from Section 1.1. These contributions are our event model, our event processing language and the system implementing them. Further contributions are the adherence to Web standards and expressive software tooling to foster adoption of our approach. Our contributions are as follows:

1. *An **event model** based on RDF.* Our event model is an expressive RDF schema. It supports arbitrarily structured events unlike flat or atomic schemas found in large parts of the related work. On the

other hand, our format is suitable for event processing unlike some schemas which allow fuzzy temporal properties which cannot be processed by machines. Moreover, our schema is designed with interoperability as a goal and fosters re-use of domain schemas.

2. *An **event pattern language** based on RDF and SPARQL.* Our language has support for combined (hybrid) patterns of real-time data and historic data using transparent joins built into the language whereas existing languages can query historic data mostly by imperative, non-declarative extensions or not at all.
3. *Design and Software Implementation of our **event processing system*** to process the event model and patterns.
4. *Use of open **Web standards*** for event modelling, pattern modelling, access control.
5. *Software **tooling**:* SDK for event modelling and event-based communication, event adapters for existing sources (Twitter, Facebook, Xively).

These contributions collectively address the research questions stated in Section 1.1 and thus show how the Web can be made situation-aware when data is on the move using push-oriented communication.

1.4. Previous Publications

The core contributions of this thesis are peer-reviewed and published as follows. For each of the core contributions (model, pattern language and system) we will select one most viable publication.

Event Model: The RDF event model elaborated in Chapter 5 is described in [Stühmer et al. 2009a] and [Stühmer et al. 2009b] and was demonstrated in [Stühmer et al. 2009c]. The most important publication for the event model was presented at the *8th International Semantic Web Conference (ISWC 2009)* [Stühmer et al. 2009b]:

> Roland Stühmer, Darko Anicic, Sinan Sen, Jun Ma, Kay-Uwe Schmidt, and Nenad Stojanovic [2009b]. 'Lifting events

in RDF from interactions with annotated Web pages'. In: *The Semantic Web - ISWC 2009*. Vol. 5823. Lecture Notes in Computer Science. Springer Berlin / Heidelberg, pp. 893–908. ISBN: 978-3-642-04929-3. DOI: {10.1007/978-3-642-04930-9_56}.

Event Pattern Language: The language BDPL elaborated in Chapter 6 was first described in [Stojanovic et al. 2012] and evaluated for performance in [Stojanovic et al. 2013]. The most important publication for BDPL was presented in our paper at the *7th ACM International Conference on Distributed Event-Based Systems (DEBS 2013)* [Stojanovic et al. 2013]:

Nenad Stojanovic, Ljiljana Stojanovic, and Roland Stühmer [2013]. 'Tutorial: Personal Big Data Management in Cyber-physical Systems – The Role of Event Processing'. In: *Proceedings of the 7th ACM international conference on Distributed event-based systems*. New York, NY, USA. ISBN: 978-1-4503-1758-0. DOI: 10.1145/2488222.2488348.

System: The overall system elaborated in Chapter 7 was presented at the *14th IFIP Working Conference on Virtual Enterprises (PRO-VE 2013)* and is published in [Stühmer et al. 2013]:

Roland Stühmer, Yiannis Verginadis, Iyad Alshabani, Thomas Morsellino, and Antonio Aversa [2013]. 'PLAY: Semantics-Based Event Marketplace'. In: *14th IFIP Working Conference on Virtual Enterprise – Special Session on Event-Driven Collaborative Networks*. Ed. by Luis M. Camarinha-Matos and Raimar J. Scherer. Vol. 408. IFIP Advances in Information and Communication Technology. Springer, pp. 699–707. DOI: 10.1007/978-3-642-40543-3_73.

Moreover, we published the general motivation for using **Semantic Web technologies** in event processing [Stojanovic et al. 2011] and more specifically using **Linked Data** in event processing [Wagner et al. 2010].

The research challenges have been discussed in a doctoral consortium at the *4th ACM International Conference on Distributed Event-Based Systems (DEBS 2010)*.

Finally, our approach is evaluated in previously published works on the **use cases** of crisis management [Barthe-Delanoë et al. 2012], [Truptil et al. 2012] and logistics [Lauras et al. 2012].

1.5. Guide to the Reader

This thesis is structured as follows. Chapters 1 to 4 are preliminaries, Chapters 5 to 7 are the three main chapters referring to the main contributions and addressing the three research questions. Chapters 8 to 9 present evaluation and conclusions only followed by appendices, bibliography and the index at the end of this document.

Chapter 1, *Introduction*, posed the research questions under the principal question: *How can the Web be made situation-aware?*

Chapter 2, *Requirements*, breaks down the questions into tractable requirements for designing the final artefacts as contributions of this thesis.

Chapters 3 and 4, *Foundations* and *State of the Art* describe related work. Foundations are work which is related "vertically" to this work being underpinnings or technology necessary for an understanding when reading this thesis. State of the Art on the other hand is related work with similar goals and/or similar applications to this thesis where a comparative analysis is conducted.

Chapters 5 to 7, *A Model for Events*, *A Pattern Language for Events* and *An Infrastructure for Events* describe the main contributions of this thesis. The research questions and their requirements are addressed there. Resulting models, methods and instantiations are described.

Chapter 8, *Evaluation*, evaluates the artefacts produced as part of this work. Qualitative comparisons are made with the State of the Art and the overall cost of the Web-based approach is determined quantitatively and compared to a non-Web-based solution.

Chapter 9, *Conclusions and Outlook*, summarises the results, discusses their significance and points to future work.

Appendices, the bibliography and the index conclude this document.

2

Requirements

In this chapter we dive deeper into the design of the main contributions of this thesis. To that end we elaborate on finer-grained requirements stemming from the research questions from Section 1.1. Each research question is broken down into tractable requirements for the further design of the contributions. Research Question 1 (Web Interoperability) is discussed in Sections 2.1 to 2.3. Research Question 2 (Processing Language) is discussed in Section 2.4. Finally, Research Question 3 (Infrastructure) is discussed in Sections 2.5 to 2.7. The requirements collected here are revisited in the main chapters and evaluation chapter below to measure the results.

2.1. Requirements for Event Modelling (Event Format)

Let us remind ourselves of the first research question:

Research Question 1 (Web Interoperability). *How can we achieve event interoperability for situation awareness at a Web scale?*

The question addresses data modelling specific to events and moreover specific to the Web. First, we collect requirements specific to events in this section. Thereafter, we collect requirements for the Web and more specifically Linked Data in subsequent sections below.

An event is something that happens, or is contemplated as happening within a particular system or domain [Etzion and Niblett 2010]. Events are first-class objects, i.e. a fundamental information unit. This means they can be stored, queried and merged with other events [Gupta and Jain 2011] and do not need to be inferred from changes in state or in class membership or in other implicit means. Moreover, in many real-life systems the number of different states is quite large and cannot be modelled at design time [Gupta and Jain 2011, Section 2.3]. This requires a model which explicitly models the known and relevant relationships, i.e. events, instead of all possible states and state transitions.

Requirement R1: Events are first-class objects
Events are first-class objects, they are a fundamental information unit which can be stored, queried and merged with other events. Events explicitly model the known relationships in an application domain.

According to [Gupta and Jain 2011, Chapter 2] important properties of an event are time, a type-hierarchy and inter-event relationships to make events more meaningful. Consequently the next requirements are to support time properties and type-hierarchies.

Requirement R2: Time properties
Time properties of events must be supported.

Requirement R3: Type hierarchy
Type hierarchies of events must be supported.

In [Etzion and Niblett 2010, Section 3.4] and [Gupta and Jain 2011, Sections 2.3 and 3.2] required relationships between events are specified as membership, generalization, specialization and retraction. The relation *membership* between two events means that one event can be a member in another event when one event caused the other event, or was used in the detection and inference of the other. The relations of *generalization* and *specialization* resemble the known object-oriented notions of superclass and subclass for event classes which are more general or less general than other classes. The relation of *retraction*, finally, is used to model events which retract the facts conveyed by previous events. Since events are often treated as being immutable [Luckham and Schulte 2011] (cf. Section 3.6), an event cannot be deleted but a retraction can be sent.

Requirement R4: Inter-event relationships
Inter-event relationships must be supported.

Semantic Web technologies such as RDF provide re-usable schemas, called ontologies. An ontology is a "formal, explicit specification of a shared conceptualisation" [Studer et al. 1998]. Sharing of a conceptualisation is done to enable interoperability between systems and datasets. Thus, interoperability can be achieved through common ontologies [Pinto and Martins 2000]. This leads to the requirement for ontology re-use.

Requirement R5: Ontology re-use
Classes and properties from existing ontologies must be re-used where possible to increase interoperability.

2.2. Web Requirements

A growing number of resources on the Web move away from traditional request/response communication. Examples include not just Twitter but broader technologies such as WebHooks, Callbacks, HTML5, WebSockets and movements such as the Internet of Things (IoT). We explain these examples in more detail in Sections 3.9 and 3.10.

The reason we mention these examples here is that a lot of push-data is already available on the Web today. Such data sources can be leveraged to alleviate a cold start of our approach as well as demonstrate interoperability with existing systems. This leads us to the next requirement:

Requirement R6: Push-data on the Web
Bottom-up movements on the Web such as available and upcoming push-data initiatives must be leveraged to acquire and process data.

2.3. Linked Data Requirements

The Linked Data principles [Berners-Lee 2006] are a methodology for publishing structured data on the Web and to interlink the data to make them more useful. (Cf. Section 3.1.) The principles were described and implemented for static data.

For streaming data, on the other hand, there are no separate guidelines. Such data, however, could also profit from the aforementioned principles and the principles apply just as well. This leads us to the next requirement:

Requirement R7: Linked Data Principles for Modelling
The Linked Data principles must be employed for modelling events and static data using HTTP URIs and outgoing links.

To exchange events we need a method of streaming the data. Addressing the Linked Data principles, therefore, we require an RDF Streaming API to adapt the four Linked Data principles to real-time applications.

While the event format is built on top of RDF as required above the *data modelling* language thus fits seamlessly with the *data distribution* via RDF streams:

Requirement R8: Linked Data Principles for Publishing
The Linked Data principles must be employed for publishing events and static data using dereferenceable URIs.

2.4. Requirements for Event Processing (Pattern Language)

Let us recall the next research question:

Research Question 2 (Processing Language). *How to design and realise a processing language for Web events?*

This question addresses a real-time processing language tailored to the use on Web events. Events are modelled according to the requirements stated above. To process events a language is needed which is a close fit to the data model used for these events. This leads us to the first requirement for the language:

Requirement R9: Support for the data model
The processing language must be suitable for the data model.

Event processing often focuses on the detection of patterns in event streams in real-time using *in-memory techniques*. However, for supporting longer-term data analysis archived streams are necessary [Dindar et al. 2011]. The number of use cases of a language is greatly increased by enabling queries for both real-time and historic events/data. It is a design goal of this work to allow both types of data in the same query resulting in hybrid queries:

Requirement R10: Hybrid Querying
The query language must support mixed queries comprised of both real-time and historic events.

Our event processing language must support typical temporal operators. Temporal operators are employed by event processing systems to relate two or more events to each other. Typical examples are a sequence which matches two events in the right order [Etzion and Niblett 2010, Section 9.3.1] or time windows which match zero or more events whose timestamps fall within the interval of the time window.

Some streaming systems (cf. Section 4.2) do not offer temporal operators. Instead, users are required to emulate temporal semantics manually, using arithmetic on timestamps. Apart from being complicated and unnecessarily verbose, manual time arithmetic is error-prone and not portable. Explicit temporal operators on the other hand may be overloaded to deal with interval-based and point-based events interchangeably. Using overloading, e.g. our sequence operators are able to process events with just one timestamp and events with two timestamps (intervals) transparently without the query author having to write conditional statements. This results in shorter and more complete queries. All possible interval-based relationships are described in [Allen 1981]. Event processing systems must be able to detect these relationships by offering matching temporal operators:

Requirement R11: Temporal Operators
The query language must support typical temporal operators.

2.5. Event Processing Grand Challenge

Let us recall the third and final research question:

Research Question 3 (Infrastructure). *How to design and develop an efficient infrastructure supporting a Web of events?*

This question deals with infrastructure which is needed to support situation awareness on the Web. Exchanging data in real-time requires special infrastructure, so does the enforcement of privacy guarantees in the Real-time Web. We collect all our requirements in this section with the help of other people who postulated these requirements before us.

The Real-time Web is the notion of an Web-scale network where information is exchanged in a push fashion as opposed to the mostly request/response oriented Web where information must be *requested* first before it can be consumed. In the Real-time Web information is pushed to the consumer based on her/his interests in real-time as soon as the information is created. The goals of such an event-driven Web are quicker reactions to important news and possibly proactivity by greater information awareness.

The Real-time Web is defined in [Chandy et al. 2011] through a set of challenges. The event processing community[1] defines a so-called grand challenge serving as *a common goal and mechanism for coordinating research across the spectrum of people working on event processing*. The document identifies *a single, though broad challenge that impacts society* and at the same time *provides a basis for measuring progress of the EP community*.

The grand challenge in event processing [Chandy et al. 2011] lists the requirements for creating a Real-time Web. The challenge is defined there as a "fabric into which components can be easily plugged and unplugged, enabling the development of time-driven or event-based global applications".

The challenge particularises that an (i) infrastructure is needed using (ii) widely-accepted open standards which (iii) enables time-driven or event-driven applications and furthermore is (iv) "on-the-fly adaptive". This leads us to the next four requirements:

Requirement R12: Infrastructure
Infrastructure must be provided.

Requirement R13: Open Standards
Widely-accepted open standards must be used.

Requirement R14: Event-driven
Time-driven or event-driven applications must be enabled.

Requirement R15: Adaptivity
Adaptivity on-the-fly must be supported for changing event models and for changing event patterns.

2.6. Event Marketplace

In order to bring consumers and producers of events together, we envision a marketplace for events or event sources. Such a marketplace is a system where producers of events make their events known and consumers look

[1] The community is represented by vendors and scientists in the Event Processing Technical Society: http://en.wikipedia.org/wiki/Event_Processing_Technical_Society

for available events. Much like service marketplaces such a system serves as an (albeit loose) coupling of Web-scale systems. Pricing, however, a common task of marketplaces is out of the scope of this thesis.

A large marketplace will have numerous event sources which emit a high number of event streams of different event types. For a user to make sense of this, search functionality is required. To make an event marketplace work, metadata must be created and collected for event types, streams and sources:

Requirement R16: Event Metadata
Metadata must be created and collected for event types, streams and sources. The metadata must be made searchable.

Multitenancy facilitates the virtual separation of tenants in an information system. To accommodate producers and consumers of events with private data the marketplace must employ means of separating tenants from each other:

Requirement R17: Multitenancy
The system must employ means of separating tenants from each other.

2.7. Requirements from Scenarios

Our work was used in a research project on RDF-oriented event processing[2]. Two scenarios were carried out in the project. Both contributed further requirements to our work. The technical report [Benaben et al. 2013] describes the two scenarios as (i) a telecommunications use case and (ii) a crisis management use case.

The telecommunications use case simulates location-based services for smartphones in combination with social media. To that end the use case contributes a simulation environment containing event streams and event patterns. Using the simulation and a matching smartphone app the scenario can demonstrate the behaviour of many smartphone users emitting

[2]Research Project PLAY funded by the European Commission (Grant 258659) http://www.play-project.eu/

and consuming events in real-time and with location-awareness. The event sources involved in the telecommunications use case are (i) location updates of mobile phones from the simulator, (ii) phone calls from the simulator and (iii) social media updates from the Web using our event adapter described in Section 7.6. Based on these available events the use case offers location-based user recommendations on how and where to contact a certain person in the scenario.

The crisis management use case considers the simulation of a nuclear crisis situation in which a large quantity of radioactive substance is accidentally released in the atmosphere, due to a critical accident in a French nuclear plant. Simulated, heterogeneous actors have to work together with the shared aim to solve or at least improve the crisis situation. The event sources involved in the nuclear crisis scenarios are Web Services, which send and receive events in order to simulate the evolution of the crisis situation on the one hand like the radiation rate and on the other hand the dynamics of the crisis response by the simulated actors. Supporting both use cases and their scenarios leads us to the next requirement for our language:

Requirement R18: Query Expressivity
The scenarios must be supported in their query expressivity.

Supporting location-based services requires our event model to leverage event properties to define geolocations and our pattern language to process such events accordingly:

Requirement R19: Mobility
The scenarios must be supported in their need for mobile data.

The experts of both use cases needed to publish events from their sources mentioned above. However, not all programmers are trained in using technologies such as RDF and RDFS necessary for our work. Thus, it is a requirement for programmers to be able to create events without skills in RDF and RDFS:

Requirement R20: Support for Programmers
The scenarios must be supported so that programmers can easily produce events in RDF.

This concludes the collection of requirements. They are revisited during the design and implementation of the main contributions in Chapters 5 to 7 and finally for an overall picture of their fulfilment in Chapter 8.

3 Foundations

In this chapter we describe basic definitions, terms and technologies the understanding of which is helpful in reading the rest of this work. The following sections describe basics which are related to this work by being necessary building blocks. The state of the art in work comparable to ours is explained separately in the next chapter (4).

3.1. Resource Description Framework (RDF) and Linked Data

Resource Description Framework (RDF) [Klyne and Carroll 2004] and its schema language RDFS are a general method for conceptual description or modelling of information. RDF is used for making statements about resources. Statements are made in the form of subject-predicate-object expressions (triples). Triples can be extended with a fourth component (resulting in quadruples) to record the provenance of the statement.

Apart from the advantages of RDF as a data model, there is the advantage of having a lot of public data readily available in RDF that can be re-used[1]. This means that a lot of static data is available to be used as context of events. We make use of Linked Data during the implementation of a scenario in Section 8.5 where we use information about known geographical locations inside the city of Berlin to model the scenario.

Linked Data are a recommended best practice for exposing, sharing, and connecting pieces of data, information, and knowledge on the Semantic Web using URIs and RDF [Berners-Lee 2006]. The basic idea is to use dereferenceable links in RDF to improve discovery of related information on the Web.

Examples of Linked Data are geographical names and their globally unique identifiers which can be found on-line. These identifiers are useful in identity management on the Web. Publishing Linked Data in general is done using four steps [Berners-Lee 2006]:

1. **Use URIs** to identify things.
2. Use **HTTP URIs** so that these things can be referred to and looked up ("dereferenced") by people and user agents.
3. Provide **useful information** about the thing when its URI is dereferenced, using standard formats such as RDF and SPARQL.
4. **Include links** to other, related URIs in the exposed data to improve discovery of other related information on the Web.

This was described and implemented for static data. For streaming data, on the other hand, there are no similar guidelines. Streaming data could, however, also profit from the aforementioned principles and they apply just as well. We explain our solution for Linked Data streaming later in this thesis.

[1] Data Sets: http://linkeddata.org/data-sets

Standards for streaming RDF data are also not yet available. There is, however, a W3C working group on the subject, called "RDF Stream Processing Community Group"[2,3].

3.2. SPARQL Protocol and RDF Query Language

SPARQL Protocol and RDF Query Language (SPARQL) is a W3C standard to query RDF data [Harris and Seaborne 2010]. SPARQL is a SQL-like query language but supports graph-based patterns to match RDF. Unlike SQL, SPARQL supports three different query forms. Select queries, Construct queries and Ask queries. They differ in the structure of their result sets.

A **Select query** has relational results like in SQL. The result set consists of a schema of variables with a set of tuples binding these variables. The result set of a **Construct query** does not consist of arbitrary-length tuples but is in triple form like its input, thus producing RDF statements from RDF statements. In other words, a Construct query is self-mapping RDF to RDF, a useful characteristic when processing interoperable data. Finally, an **Ask query** returns a purely Boolean result depending on whether the query was matched (one or more times) or was not matched.

In this work we use all three query forms, most noticeably the Construct form in our pattern language producing RDF events (Section 6.3), the Select form in our system communicating with storage backends for static data (Section 7.2) and the Ask form validating access permissions to Boolean `true` or `false` (Section 7.3).

SPARQL queries are designed like SQL queries to be one-time queries. They are posed by a client, then answered by a database system and then discarded. However, event processing requires continuous queries. They must be monitored by a system continuously matching events whenever

[2]W3C RDF Stream Processing Community Group: http://www.w3.org/community/rsp/
[3]The author of this thesis is a member of the group.

they happen. To that end, our Construct queries (Section 6.3) are interpreted in a continuous fashion. Related work on continuous SPARQL is discussed in Section 4.2.

3.3. REST versus SOAP

Representational state transfer (REST) and Simple Object Access Protocol (SOAP) are two competing standards and best practises to model Web Services.

SOAP[4] heavily relies on XML to model structured information in Web Services. A stack of protocols is defined to implement various aspects of communication in XML such as security. The protocols may define and extend the capabilities of a Web Service defining actions in an arbitrary manner.

REST[5] relies on the limited set of "verbs" from HTTP 1.1 to describe actions which can be performed on URLs. Examples are get, put, delete and post. REST is not an official protocol like SOAP but rather an architectural style on modelling services using basic technologies such as HTTP.

In this work we use both SOAP and REST where applicable. SOAP is used, e.g. in Section 7.1.2 where a *standardised* protocol for the exchange of events is needed. REST on the other hand is used in this work, e.g. in Section 7.4 where *simplicity* is needed for the design of a new service.

3.4. Push versus Pull

Many data sources are accessed in a pull fashion. This means that a request for data has to be initiated by the client and is answered by the server providing the data source. Communication is bipartite in that there are

[4]W3C SOAP: http://www.w3.org/TR/soap/
[5]REST: http://www.ics.uci.edu/~fielding/pubs/dissertation/rest_arch_style.htm

two kinds of messages: requests and responses. Most information systems such as databases work in this way. Most of the Web works in this way.

However, request/response is not an optimal solution to the problem of *timely* data dissemination: Data sources must be polled regularly and clients must check the polling result for possible updates. This means that the polling interval (chosen by the client) influences the perceived "real-time" behaviour of an application: A long interval results in new items being received late, a very long interval can even result in lost updates[6]. A very short interval on the other hand results in inefficiency for both client and server because many costly calls are being made with no new results.

The drawbacks of pulling data [Martin-Flatin 1999] can best be mitigated by introducing push-oriented architectures [Mühl et al. 2006, p. 17]. There, the server chooses when communication is initiated. This usually happens when new data is available avoiding unnecessary communication and disseminating updates in a timely fashion.

3.5. Publish/Subscribe

Publish/subscribe is a messaging pattern for push-based communication. Producers and consumers are decoupled from each other in that no hard-coded connections between them are formed. Instead, messages are *published* by producers regardless of the consumer (i.e. the type of consumer, the time of consumption, the number of consumers or varying consumers over time). Consumers, on the other hand, express their interest in messages by issuing *subscriptions* for certain messages. A publish/subscribe system is further characterised by the expressivity of the subscriptions it supports:

[6]Lost updates occur in the case of aggregate feeds such as RSS which only return the latest n items (e.g. 40 most recent entries). A client using a very long polling interval might poll again after $n + x$ items are created but the feed only returns n latest items resulting in the loss of items for the client.

Topic-based Publish/Subscribe: Messages can be organised into subjects by the producer [Mühl et al. 2006, Section 2.3.2]. These subjects (so-called "topics") are usually annotated as metadata on each message. A subscription can then ask for only certain messages of one or more topics. In this way messages can be filtered based on metadata. Thus, the topics define virtual channels. Topic-based publish/subscribe is the most widely[7] used form of publish/subscribe. It is quite expressive but still relatively efficient compared to content-based publish/subscribe described below. The downside of topic-based publish/subscribe is that the virtual channels formed by topics are mostly governed by the publisher thus restricting the expressivity of filtering for the consumer. Content-based publish/subscribe mitigates this shortcoming.

Content-based Publish/Subscribe: Instead of filtering for message metadata, content-based publish/subscribe can filter based on properties inside the message payload, i.e. looking into the message body [Mühl et al. 2006, Section 2.3.4]. This increases the expressivity of subscriptions by enabling the consumer to classify messages regardless of the classification by the producer. Producer and consumer can thus be decoupled to a higher degree. Filtering for message content instead of metadata usually incurs higher cost at runtime, making content-based publish/subscribe systems less efficient compared to topic-based ones.

3.6. Events

An event is something that happens, or is contemplated as happening [Etzion and Niblett 2010] and events are first-class objects which means a fundamental information unit which can be stored, queried and merged with other events [Gupta and Jain 2011]. Events can be exchanged as part of messages in a push-based fashion.

[7] Supported by standards such as WS-Topics and widely implemented, e.g. by Apache ActiveMQ: http://activemq.apache.org/

We distinguish several subclasses of events. Since events can be processed in event processing systems we distinguish events which are input and output of such systems. A **simple event** (also called raw event) [Etzion and Niblett 2010, Section 2.2.1] is an event which is input to a system. A **derived event** [Ibid.] is an event which is generated as an output (result) of event processing. Delineating further, a **complex event** [Luckham and Schulte 2011] is an event that summarizes, represents, or denotes a set of other events. Finally, a **composite event** [Etzion and Niblett 2010, Section 3.2.1] is a complex event which physically contains the set of events which it summarises, represents, or denotes. With the use of Linked Data for events, however, the distinction of complex and composite events becomes blurred. A composite event using Linked Data will contain *links* to its member events and not physically repeat their data. Thus, such a composite event using Linked Data will not be distinguishable from a complex event. Therefore, throughout this work the term complex event will be sufficient.

Events can be defined over a single point in time or with a duration, i.e. an interval. **Point-based events** [Etzion and Niblett 2010, Section 11.1.1] are appropriate when describing state transitions which have no duration. In reality, however, many events happen over a period of time [Ibid.]. Moreover, the detection of complex events happens over a period of time, so **interval-based events** can be used to describe the results. Using time-point semantics when detecting complex events has non-intuitive effects on the semantics of such simple notions as a sequence[8] [Galton and Augusto 2002, Section 4].

In many event processing systems **events are immutable** [Luckham and Schulte 2011]. This stems from the definition of an event as *something that happens*, meaning an event cannot be made to unhappen. Immutability

[8]The authors of [Galton and Augusto 2002] for example point out that the sequence patterns "$\rightarrow$" of three events $E_1 \rightarrow (E_2 \rightarrow E_3)$ and $E_2 \rightarrow (E_1 \rightarrow E_3)$ both match the same sequence of events e_1, e_2, e_3 contrary to an intuitive understanding of sequences. This happens if time points and not intervals are used to represent the results of the parentheses: The last time point in the parenthesis is used which is always e_3 regardless of the other event in the parenthesis. Thus, the parenthesis fulfils the sequence operator in some unexpected cases.

is a valuable assumption when building event processing systems; especially, when employing publish/subscribe communication. There, several receivers may obtain a copy of the same event and continue processing it. The loose coupling of the agents involved makes is hard to guarantee consistency between the distributed data (i.e. copies of events). Thus, the guarantee for immutability is helpful.

Instead of altering events, **event retraction** [Etzion and Niblett 2010, Section 11.3.1] may be used: Many systems with event immutability offer to send a so-called retraction event referring to an old event which occurred previously (e.g. [Aničić 2012]). Upon retraction, the older event is not deleted from an information systems standpoint but is said to be retracted by the presence of the retraction event. The subsequent state of the old event being retracted (but still available) in a system is similar to a notion from temporal database research where data can have a transaction-time and a possibly shorter valid-time.

Apart from deleting events, immutability also affects other operations manipulating events, for example enriching events with more data or projecting events to drop unneeded properties. Event processing systems deal with this issue by stipulating that **derived events have a new identity**. Therefore, new, derived events are created and the original, simple events remain unchanged. Optionally, such derived events may contain a reference to the original, unaltered event to maintain provenance.

Historic events [Etzion and Niblett 2010, Section 6.4] and other static reference data must be distinguished from events. Such data is needed in event processing systems, e.g. to enrich events or otherwise help if more data is needed than is contained in an event. Historic data is exchanged in a pull-based fashion.

3.7. Event Processing Systems

Event processing is defined as *computing that performs operations on events, including reading, creating, transforming, or discarding events* [Luckham and

Schulte 2011]. Since events are the fundamental unit of information, each event is processed atomically, i.e. completely or not at all.

Much like database management relies on database management systems; event processing relies on event processing systems. The ingredients of event processing are the events (data), event patterns (queries) and processing engines (systems). The ingredients are typically combined in an architecture called event processing network (EPN) [Etzion and Niblett 2010, Section 2.2].

Event processing systems offer a certain granularity as to how events can be processed. If a system offers operators to group events in sets and then operate on them using set-oriented operators (e.g. aggregation functions such as min, max, count), a system is said to support set-at-a-time semantics. If a system supports per-event operators (e.g. detection of a sequence of two specific events), the system is said to support event-at-a-time semantics. Distinguishing these two notions marked the advent of *event processing systems* supporting both types of semantics whereas *stream processing systems* support only sets, i.e. after grouping events into sets of events[9]. For the remainder of this work, the distinction of both semantics is interesting with regards to the expressivity of supported operators in an event processing system or its language.

Event processing systems are available today as re-usable products, commercially or open-source. However, most systems take a closed-domain approach to modelling such that, e.g. the supported events are defined in one place, by a limited number of people, for a known domain. In our work we target an open world with many people defining event schemas and supporting privacy, i.e. access control on streams amongst these users.

Also, the popular streaming frameworks such as Apache Storm[10] and Apache S4[11] provide only a framework for processing data. They do

[9] The two approaches were previously called complex event processing (CEP) vs. event stream processing (ESP) which are other terms for the same disambiguation.

[10] Apache Storm, formerly Twitter Storm: http://storm-project.net/

[11] Apache S4, formerly Yahoo S4: http://incubator.apache.org/s4/

not define event operators on a declarative level neither set-at-a-time nor event-at-a-time.

3.8. Event Formats

In a heterogeneous system such as the Web, a common understanding of data exchanged is crucial. According to [Rozsnyai et al. 2007b] this is especially true in a decoupled system such as an event-based system where the producer and consumer of an event might have no knowledge of each other. Therefore, a consumer must find a way to understand received events which entails the need for a universal event model [Rozsnyai et al. 2007b].

Many event-based systems such as Gryphon [Aguilera et al. 1999], Siena [Carzaniga et al. 2001], Hermes [Pietzuch and Bacon 2002] and Padres [Fidler et al. 2005] use very simple event models, i.e. only list-based event schemata or key/value pairs, modelling purely syntactical data where semantics must be derived from its values. The attribute types belong to a predefined set of primitive types found in common programming languages. Some attempts were made to define a universal vocabulary for events. A notable approach from industry is the WSDM Event Format (WEF) standardised by OASIS [Kreger 2005]. The standard is extensible and contains some predefined XML elements for the event domain of reporting situations in *IT systems monitoring*, creating some level of agreement on what these terms mean to a sender and a receiver of such events. An approach from research is the XML format of AMIT presented in [Adi et al. 2000]. It goes beyond the previous approaches, e.g. by providing more detailed temporal semantics and by modelling not only events but generalization, specialization and other relationships between events which can be used in processing.

While designing an event-based system at Web scale, it is useful to employ widely available Semantic Web Technologies to model events as proposed in [Stojanovic et al. 2011], such as RDF. Previous efforts using RDF were made in [Petrovic et al. 2005] and [Qian et al. 2008]. RDF and its schema language RDFS are well suited for distributed Web-scale exchange of data (in our case events) between inhomogeneous systems. We discuss RDF-oriented formats in detail in Section 4.1.

3.9. Protocols for Real-time Data on the Web

There are many technological developments on the Web today which create events. Such events are delivered in a push fashion as opposed to the traditional client–server Web of request and response.

Technologies such as AJAX [Garrett 2005] and Comet [Russell 2006] are widely used to enable push-data from the server to the client. However, push transfer is in many cases only achieved by the client polling a server. To emulate real-time behaviour, the server answers the poll only when new data becomes available and blocking the call otherwise until data is available. Since the client poll is then fulfilled (i.e. the call returns), the client must poll again for further data. The described mechanism of blocking a call until data becomes available and then polling again is called long-polling. Another disadvantage is that client-side logic in JavaScript is required for the approach to function. Other approaches without the mentioned drawbacks are available or upcoming.

For one, there is the W3C Web Notification Working Group[12] which is working on push notifications to actively notify running Web applications in browsers. Additionally, HTML5 defines two techniques to facilitate communication initiated by the server. These techniques are *Server-Sent Events*[13] and *WebSockets*[14]. They operate on different layers of the protocol stack to achieve push delivery to Web clients.

RSS and other news feed formats offer schemas for publishing frequently updated information. However, they are not a solution to the problem of *timely* data dissemination because they rely on pull (cf. Section 3.4). The

[12] Web Notification Working Group: http://www.w3.org/2010/06/notification-charter
[13] Server-Sent Events: http://www.w3.org/TR/eventsource/
[14] WebSocket API: http://www.w3.org/TR/websockets/

intrinsic drawbacks apply to all feed-oriented applications such as Yahoo Pipes[15].

Google *PubSubHubbub* protocol[16] is designed to mitigate inefficient pulling of news feeds in Atom or RSS. To that end, PubSubHubbub provides a push-oriented protocol based on WebHooks[17]. Today it is mainly used to enable server-to-server notifications. Further server-to-server techniques are WebHooks themselves, Pingback[18] and Semantic Pingback[19].

Lastly, the Facebook Graph API provides an application-specific way to subscribe to real-time updates[20] from changes to connected people's profiles.

The amount of existing and upcoming protocols provides motivation for real-time infrastructures on the Web such as undertaken by this work. Apart from technical underpinnings for this work there are applications on the Web which provide content which can be consumed in real-time. We will describe such data sources next.

3.10. Data Sources for Real-time Data on the Web

Social Web sites such as Facebook and Twitter host a large amount of user-contributed material for a wide variety of events happening in the real-world. Events from Xively[21] further extend this range of events by adding real-time data from devices around the world which people are sharing.

[15] Yahoo Pipes: http://pipes.yahoo.com

[16] Google PubSubHubbub protocol http://code.google.com/p/pubsubhubbub/

[17] WebHooks: http://www.webhooks.org/

[18] Pingback: http://www.hixie.ch/specs/pingback/pingback

[19] Semantic Pingback: http://aksw.org/Projects/SemanticPingBack

[20] Facebook Graph API Real-time Updates http://developers.facebook.com/docs/api/realtime

[21] Xively, a Web portal to connect sensor data: http://xively.com/ previously known as Cosm and before that as Pachube

Such data sources do not offer a common interface to receive real-time data. After all, there are no standards-based ways to exchange real-time data on the Web. However, application-specific adapters can be created to connect to these sources. We do this in Section 7.6. Consequently, we can consume real-time data from the Web in our infrastructure.

4 State of the Art

After having discussed related work of underlying foundations in the previous chapter we now discuss related work which is comparable to this work.

4.1. RDF Event Models

Widely available Semantic Web technologies are a good match for modelling events in a Web-oriented, event-based system [Sen and Stojanovic 2010]. RDF and its schema language RDFS are well suited for distributed Web-scale exchange of data (in our case events) between inhomogeneous systems through the re-use of shared schemas.

Some RDF-based event formats such as [Gutierrez et al. 2007] use time as a second-class citizen. This means that temporal properties are handled implicitly by the system, e.g. by maintaining hidden timestamps for each RDF triple, i.e. using quintuples internally. Several current RDF streaming systems work in the same way, cf. C-SPARQL, EP-SPARQL, Linked Data-Fu and Sparkwave described in the following section. These systems define an event as one triple and define a stream as a series of triples. Since one triple can contain just one statement there is no event model which can hold multiple properties of an event such as a type, a timestamp or other event metadata.

However, there are schemas similar to ours in that they model events as larger graphs consisting of more than one triple per event. This allows for time as a first-class citizen in one or more triples contained in the event graph. Such schemas include E* [Gupta and Jain 2011], F [Scherp et al. 2009] and LODE [Shaw et al. 2009], all of which also rely on the DOLCE [Gangemi et al. 2002] top-level ontology as we do. However, they do not seem to be tailored to real-time processing of events because a lot of their (e.g. temporal) expressivity such as relative and vague time is not supported by the state of the art in real-time processing engines. Therefore, these event models remain partly theoretical.

The authors of the RDF streaming system INSTANS describe a more elaborated event model in a workshop paper [Rinne et al. 2013]. The model eliminates much of the shortcomings of other approaches described above such as using tractable temporal expressiveness. However, even though several timestamps are supported with different semantics (e.g. real-world occurrence, detection time by the system, etc.) the approach does not allow interval-based semantics for describing events with a duration.

Our event format combines a large part of the expressivity and flexibility of the aforementioned formats with the execution model of our underlying processing engine ETALIS [Aničić 2012, Part II].

4.2. RDF Streaming Systems

Early efforts in RDF Streaming were made by [Petrovic et al. 2005] and [Qian et al. 2008]. Both do not focus on expressive query languages like

SPARQL but proved the feasibility of RDF-oriented event filtering to match subscriptions.

A more expressive approach, C-SPARQL is a language and a system to process streaming RDF data incrementally with more complex queries [Barbieri et al. 2010]. There, the authors define events as RDF triples. Timestamps are attached to the triples implicitly when the events enter the system. Sets of events are matched in windows. This means that the approach has a set-at-a-time semantics. The same holds true for similar approaches $\text{SPARQL}_{\text{Stream}}$ [Calbimonte et al. 2010] and CQELS [Le-Phuoc et al. 2011].

EP-SPARQL [Aničić 2012, Chapter 11] is built on top of the Prolog-based event processing engine ETALIS like our work. EP-SPARQL supports more event processing operators than C-SPARQL including event-at-a-time operators like the sequence of two events which require no mandatory window definition and are thus more declarative. Like C-SPARQL, however, this approach considers events as triples not as objects with further structure. This means that, e.g. time is a second-class citizen and not part of the event to be transmitted across distributed systems. Our approach (introduced in Chapter 5) works with structured events consisting of many RDF triples per event as opposed to one triple per event.

In addition to real-time data both C-SPARQL and EP-SPARQL can combine stream results with background knowledge. However, they do not propose a federated system to address the volume of such data. As such they are limited to static data fitting into memory on one system. Our approach integrates static data from distributed RDF stores. Queries are federated to combine data from more than one external source. Thus, we are not limited to background knowledge fitting into memory. To enable federated querying in our approach historic data is partitioned in streams. Streams are stored in distributed quad stores. Linked Data based on stream URIs is used to identify and locate the streams. This enables us to accommodate growing histories of events and other large static data sets as background knowledge.

Linked Data-Fu [Stadtmüller et al. 2013] is an RDF-oriented production rule system to derive RDF triples based on existing triples. Linked Data-Fu evaluates rules similar to Datalog using the Rete algorithm. This means that no temporal event operators are supported and no garbage collection of unconsumed triples is possible. We have previously discussed the drawbacks of using Rete for event processing in [Schmidt et al. 2008, Section 3].

INSTANS [Rinne et al. 2012] is another Rete-oriented streaming system. It uses SPARQL as a query language. The system suffers from the same drawbacks of Rete mentioned above. Also, temporal operators such as windows are not part of the language and thus must be emulated in complicated FILTER statements. Apart from being complicated and unnecessarily verbose, manual time arithmetic in a FILTER statement is error-prone and not portable. Explicit temporal operators on the other hand can be overloaded to deal with interval-based and point-based events. Our approach of *extending* SPARQL with event processing operators as first-class elements thus yields shorter and more readable queries.

Sparkwave [Komazec et al. 2012] is yet another Rete-oriented streaming system for RDF data. Sparkwave is very efficient at evaluating production rules incrementally in a forward-chaining manner on fast arriving RDF triples. Like Linked Data-Fu, Sparkwave is well suited for creating data-driven applications with real-time results. However, temporal operators are limited due to the underlying Rete algorithm which processes data purely in a set-oriented fashion disregarding any order in the arrival and validity of the data. Incorporating temporal ordering, however, is important for temporal expressivity such as detecting sequences and it is important for implementation purposes when realising efficient garbage collection.

4.3. Combining real-time with historical Querying

Real-time event processing systems today operate on pushed notifications, e.g. for changes in data. This means that data comes to the searcher. In such a setting continuous real-time queries offer insight into the data, i.e. filter, enrich, combine and otherwise process real-time data to make them useful for the searcher. However, real-time notifications often do not contain all necessary data, e.g. are missing context which must be found elsewhere. Typically, context can be retrieved through one-time, non-continuous queries.

To combine real-time and "historic" queries we propose a hybrid language called Big Data Processing Language (BDPL). A previous approach trying to achieve a similar goal is described in [Rozsnyai et al. 2007a] where queries are implicitly rewritten to also return results from "related" events, thus broadening the query along implicit event relationships. In our approach we want to make these relationships more explicit. Doing so will enable the user to join real-time data with historical data along any dimension such as time, place or domain-specific dimensions and also with non-event data increasing the expressivity of the approach.

In [Dindar et al. 2011] a real-time processing system is described which supports a language explicitly combining real-time and historic parts as BDPL in this work. However, their approach requires fixed specifications of "recency" in a query meaning that the approach is not as flexible as possible in terms of the historic part. None of the related approaches uses RDF (Linked Data) to link events with historic data.

4.4. Lambda Architecture

In [Marz and Warren 2015][1] another approach is described to combine real-time data with historic data. The book proposes the so-called Lambda Architecture. The architecture is split into two specialised systems called (i) the "speed layer" to process low-latency data (i.e. events) on the one hand and (ii) the "batch layer" for high-latency data (i.e. historic data) on the other hand. Separate systems are used for the layers with the goal of applying optimised processing logic in each case. Queries may use data from both systems simultaneously to generate answers which cover both analytic, historic aspects and real-time results.

[1] Early Access Edition, final book to appear in 2015.

Our system architecture which pre-dates the book uses a similar separation of components for event processing and storage (cf. Section 7.1) while supporting homogeneous queries against both types of data simultaneously.

4.5. RDF Access Control

There are previous approaches to modelling access control using RDF. The approaches use RDF as a modelling language for permissions linking users with user's rights on the one hand and on the other hand are used on RDF data granting access to users (linking permissions with data). All approaches *grant* access to RDF resources while assuming what is not granted is forbidden.

The S4AC Vocabulary Specification 0.2 [Villata et al. 2011] defines access rights tailored towards RDF query answering, i.e. SPARQL processing. The vocabulary defines access rights Create, Read, Update and Delete. The model is very expressive by allowing fine-grained access conditions modelled as contextual queries against arbitrary context data to check. However, the integration with SPARQL is not applicable for our system as not all operations require a query such as a plain subscription to a stream.

SIOC Access is a part of the SIOC specification [Berrueta 2010]. It is a very simple but extensible vocabulary to define permissions in the scope of the social Web. The vocabulary does not have any predefined rights. The lack of rights, the focus on social communities and its lack of traction on the Web are the drawbacks of this candidate when choosing a model for access control in our system.

The W3C WebAccessControl (WAC) [Berners-Lee 2009] is a generic vocabulary declaring some predefined rights (Read, Write, Append, Control) on Web information resources. Streams in our system are information resources so the vocabulary can be used without change. Access rights must be extended for our system to govern the real-time access `Notify` and `Subscribe` in addition to the predefined rights `Read` and `Write` for static data.

4.6. Relationship with EP-SPARQL

BDPL is in some ways similar to EP-SPARQL [Aničić 2012, Chapter 11] in that both languages describe event processing systems which have event-at-a-time and set-at-a-time (cf. Section 3.7) operators. In fact, BDPL and EP-SPARQL rely on the same underlying engine ETALIS [Anicic et al. 2009] to provide some of the temporal event detection semantics.

However, BDPL is different from EP-SPARQL in having (i) more expressive events using graphs vs. triples, (ii) a richer language using many new operators such as XPath, (iii) a clear syntactic distinction between the real-time and historic parts of the query and finally (iv) a system for federated query execution allowing distributed triple stores for historic data vs. the relatively small amount which can be held in memory by one Prolog instance.

5 A Model for Events

As the first contribution of this thesis we devise an event model for use on the Web. To that end we explain why a model is needed. Then we design the model based on the collected requirements. After that we show how this model can be used in applications by providing practical software around the model. Finally, we discuss the design decisions made.

5.1. Introduction: An open Event Model

Why do we need an event model? Some RDF streaming systems discussed in Section 4.2 have little or no model for the real-time data they ingest. These systems make the lowest common assumptions about the structure of the data, i.e. that the data consist of a stream of RDF triples. Thus, each piece of real-time data (event) is one triple. One triple, however, cannot hold a lot of information. For example when typing data, the triple `<myInstance> rdf:type <MyClass>` can introduce a type, but the event (one triple) is "full". This means that any structure in the data must be inferred from more than one event. Events, however, occur spontaneously and event consumers are often decoupled from the senders (cf. publish/subscribe in Section 3.5). Therefore, consumers cannot make assumptions about events which are not yet received.

Events should be self-describing. A common understanding of data is crucial for consumers and producers [Rozsnyai et al. 2007b], especially in a distributed and heterogeneous system such as the Web. Therefore, a consumer must find a way to understand received events which entails the need for a universal event model [Rozsnyai et al. 2007b].

5.2. Requirements

For event processing some generally accepted[1] requirements must be met. Events are objects which can be stored, queried and merged with other events, cf. Requirement R1: *Events are first-class objects*. Events have structure, cf. R2: *Time properties*, R4: *Inter-event relationships* and R3: *Type hierarchy*. According to [Cardelli 2004] "the fundamental purpose of a type system is to prevent the occurrence of execution errors during the running of a program". According to [Rozsnyai et al. 2007b] types and their description are needed in a decoupled event processing system to provide a common understanding of data. Thus, we require R16: *Event Metadata*. However, too much detail in modelling can make a model inappropriate for some of the use cases. Therefore, a balance must be found between the necessary structure of an event and the adaptivity (Requirement R15: *Adaptivity*) necessary to implement domain-specific scenarios. We collect the minimal structure for an event model such as time and types and retain extensibility of the model through requirements R13: *Open Standards*, R5: *Ontology re-use*, R7: *Linked Data Principles for Modelling* and specifically to the known scenarios: R19: *Mobility*.

[1] [Etzion and Niblett 2010; Luckham 2001; Luckham and Schulte 2011; Rozsnyai et al. 2007b; Gupta and Jain 2011]

5.2.1. The Role of Semantics

We use RDF as a modelling language for events, because it is an open standard and it is well suited for schema re-use. Using RDF has important advantages described as follows. Performance impacts at runtime are examined and described below in our evaluation, Section 8.2.

RDF is used for modelling data. Its schema language RDFS supports extensible and shared schema descriptions. These are useful in diverse, emerging scenarios such as sensor data. RDF is a standard with tooling available. This means that for modelling tasks such as creating new event schemas there is tool support available. Also, pre-existing schemas are available on the Web for immediate re-use. RDF is multi-schema friendly: This enables us to combine schemas for different applications freely and mix and match them on the fine-grained level of properties for each event type. Moreover, with RDF, schemas are optional: When complex situations are detected in our system combining more than one event, mixtures of schemas may be created implicitly and on the fly. This is not supported, e.g. by XML Schema. It follows a document-centric paradigm with mandatory schemas where the schema document must exist first. Thus, XML does not allow fine-grained re-use of schema parts in an ad-hoc fashion as RDF does. Moreover, unlike XML, RDF is self-describing[2] and can produce self-contained datasets which is useful for events which are often exchanged spontaneously and without further context. Furthermore, unlike XML, RDF allows for limited reasoning which enables event processing operations on inferred knowledge which were previously not possible in event processing. Finally, using RDF as metadata for events, streams of events, sources and actors/users provides ways of effective search and linking capabilities in an "event marketplace" infrastructure.

To create an open and extensible system, many users must be able to produce or consume events. Semantic Web mark-up can help model events. Moreover, Linked Data [Berners-Lee 2006] based on Semantic Web mark-up can help connect real-time data to static contextual data.

[2] i.e. containing both data and schema including some semantics as supported by RDFS

Such pre-existing data can be used for identity management of things, e.g. people and places. Such linkable context adds to the knowledge available when processing just a single event.

5.3. The Model

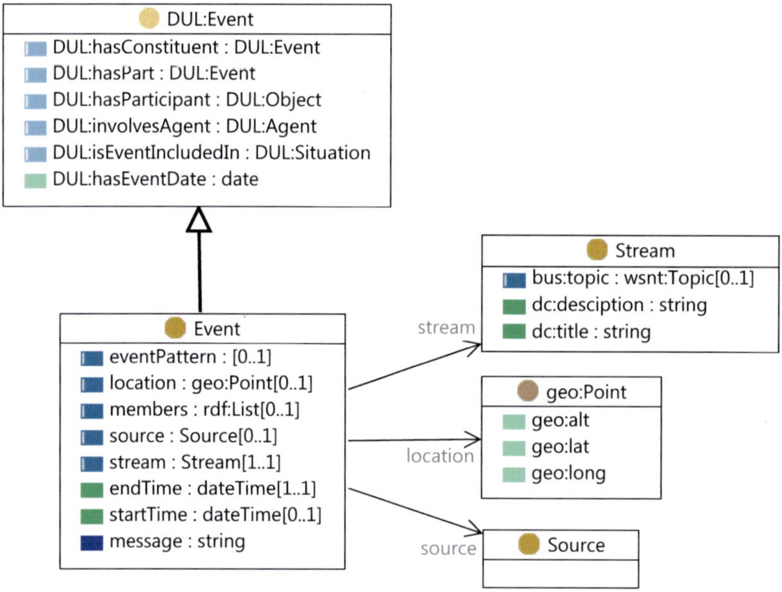

Figure 5.1.: Event Model (Class Diagram)

Figure 5.1 shows the event model in a class diagram[3]. The class "Event" at bottom left of the figure is the superclass for any event to conform to our model. This class makes use of related work by inheriting from the

[3]UML-like notation of TopBraid Composer: http://www.topquadrant.com/composer/docs/TBC-Diagram-Graph.pdf

class "DUL:Event" from Dolce Ultralight based on DOLCE [Gangemi et al. 2002]. That class provides a notion of time and helps distinguish events (things that happen) from facts (which are always valid).

In accordance with our requirements some properties are mandatory while the rest are optional. An instance of class Event MUST have (i) a type, (ii) at least one timestamp and (iii) a relevant stream. We describe the event properties in detail as follows.

The type of an event must be specified using **`rdf:type`**[4]. The type must be the class Event or any subclass. Figure 5.2 shows examples of subclasses. The hierarchy in that figure starts with the universal superclass `owl:Thing` and shows our `Event` class with domain-specific subclasses needed to implement our scenarios from Section 2.7.

The event model supports interval-based events as well as point-based events (cf. Section 3.6) by either using just the property **`:endTime`** for a point or both **`:startTime`** and `:endTime` for an interval. The property `:endTime` thus has a cardinality of `[1..1]` whereas `:startTime` has a cardinality of `[0..1]`. Both temporal properties are subproperties of `DUL:hasEventDate` from the super class. We improve the semantics by distinguishing start from end whereas the superclass has an alternative, more difficult way of formulating intervals using subobjects reifying the interval.

The property **`:stream`** associates an event with a stream. Streams are used in our system as a unit of organisation for events governing publish/subscribe (cf. Section 3.5) and access control (cf. Section 4.5). Streams themselves are modelled using title, description and a topic needed for topic-based publish/subscribe (cf. Section 3.5).

The first optional property is **`:location`**. For for geo-referencing of events (where necessary) we re-use the basic geo vocabulary from the W3C [Brickley 2003]. The property may be used to locate events in physical locations on the globe. The property is subproperty of `DUL:hasLocation` and `geo:location` to inherit the semantics from those schemas.

[4]Or using the shorthand "a" like in "is a ...". Cf. the example in Listing 5.1.

Inter-event relationships may be supported by linking a complex event to the simple events which caused it. Thus, RDF Lists may be used in `:members` to maintain an ordered and complete account of member events. The linked events are identified by their URI. These linked events could have further member events themselves. This facilitates modelling of *composite* events [Luckham and Schulte 2011]. The `:members` property is a subproperty of `DUL:hasConstituent` from the superclass.

The property `:eventPattern` may be used to link a complex event to the pattern which caused the event to be detected. Direct links to event patterns are provided by RESTful services described in Section 7.4. Using such links can help in recording provenance of derived events.

The source of an event may be specified using the `:source` property. This is an optional property to record the creator of an event where needed. The property is a subproperty of `DUL:involvesAgent`. Agents may be human or non-human.

A human readable synopsis of an event may be added using the `:message` property. This proves useful in scenarios where events are received by human end users. The `:message` property is a subproperty of `dc:title`, a popular way of describing things using natural language. Multilingualism is provided by the feature of language tags for string literals in RDF [Klyne and Carroll 2004].

N-ary predicates [Noy and Rector 2006] may be used to maintain event properties which are valid only for a specific event, e.g. a volatile sensor reading such as the temperature measurement belonging to a specific event. For example, instead of plainly stating the disputable fact that "the city of Nice has a temperature in Celsius of 23 degrees" which looks like this:

```
dbpedia:Nice :curTemp "23" .
```

We can instead state that the city of Nice has said temperature but qualified by the conjunction with a given event "e2" in the following n-ary predicate:

```
dbpedia:Nice :curTemp [
  rdf:value "23" ;
  :event <http://events...org/ids/e2#event>
] .
```

Endowment of further structure for events is left to domain-specific schemas. For example the W3C Semantic Sensor Network (SSN) Ontology[5] may be added if fine-grained modelling of sensors and pertaining sensor readings is needed.

Listing 5.1 shows several facts about our event model along an example. The listing uses the example of a Facebook event generated by our event adapter described in Section 7.6:

1. The example shows an event **using quadruples** in TriG syntax [Bizer and Cyganiak 2014]. The graph name (a.k.a context) before the curly braces is used as a unique identifier, e.g. to enable efficient indexing of contiguous triples in the storage backend for historic events.
2. The event in this example has the ID 5534987067802526 as part of its URI. There is a distinction made between **URIs for things** and URIs for their information resources, i.e. the event object `5534987067802526#event` and the Web document `5534987067802526` describing the event. The two URIs might carry, e.g. a different creation date, which is why it can be important to separate them. The fragment identifier `#event` is used to differentiate them. See [Berners-Lee 2005] for an in-depth discussion of the matter of disambiguation[6].
3. There is an **event type hierarchy** from which the type `FacebookStatusFeedEvent` is inherited. This hierarchy can be extended by any user by referencing the RDF type `:Event` as a super class. See Figure 5.2 for an example hierarchy.
4. The event may link to entities from static Linked Data where further context for the event can be retrieved. In this example the event uses `user:link` where further context for the event can be retrieved, in this case from the Facebook Graph API[7].

[5] http://www.w3.org/2005/Incubator/ssn/ssnx/ssn

[6] The issue of HTTP URIs identifying both types of resources became known as the *httpRange-14* issue after its issue number in the W3C Technical Architecture Group

[7] Facebook started publishing Linked Data as RDF [Weaver and Tarjan 2012]

5. The event links to a **stream** which is a URI where current events can be obtained in real-time by dereferencing the link.
6. The namespace `event-processing.org` is chosen as a generic home for this schema.

```
@prefix :    <http://events.event-processing.org/types/> .
@prefix e:     <http://events.event-processing.org/ids/> .
@prefix user: <http://graph.facebook.com/schema/user#> .
@prefix xsd:   <http://www.w3.org/2001/XMLSchema#> .

e:5534987067802526 {
  <http://events.event-processing.org/ids/5534987067802526#event>
    a :FacebookStatusFeedEvent ;
    :endTime "2012-03-28T06:04:26.522Z"^^xsd:dateTime ;
    :status "I bought some JEANS this morning" ;
    :stream <http://streams...org/ids/FacebookStatusFeed#stream> ;
    user:id "100000058455726" ;
    user:link <http://graph.facebook.com/roland.stuehmer#> ;
    user:location "Karlsruhe, Germany" ;
    user:name "Roland Stühmer" .
}
```

Listing 5.1: Example of an RDF Event (TriG Syntax)

We are re-using and creating domain vocabularies to subclass the class `Event`. For example in the Facebook case we use the schema from the RDF/Turtle API provided by Facebook [Weaver and Tarjan 2012].

We developed this event model to satisfy requirements of an open platform where data from the Web can be re-used and which is extensible for open participation. Future updates to the event schema can be tracked on-line at [Harth and Stühmer 2011].

5.4. Tools

In this section we describe tools which simplify dealing with our RDF event model. The tools can be roughly divided in design-time tools and run-time tools. Our contributions focus on the run-time tools, namely the software development kit (SDK) and event adapters whereas for the design-time tools users can rely on standard tools for RDF modelling.

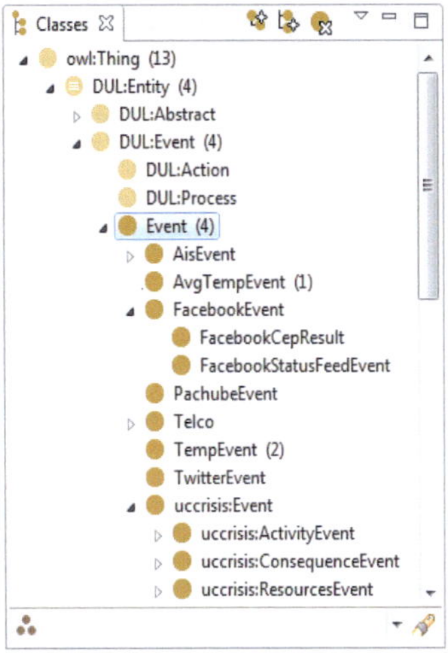

Figure 5.2.: Event Type Hierarchy

Design-Time encompasses the modelling of event classes in the schema language RDFS. For this task existing software can be used to create event classes and hierarchies. The choice for established Semantic Web Technologies such as RDF resulted in relatively good tool support. One example is TopBraid Composer[8] used in Figure 5.2.

Run-Time encompasses the creation of instances of events in RDF. However, not all programmers are skilled in Semantic Web Technologies, thus, the realisation of our scenarios required tools for the creation of events. The SDK we provide meets the Requirement R20: *Support for Programmers* in the Java programming language. We explain the aspects of the SDK to create events in more detail as follows.

Event instances conforming to our model must at least be of class "Event" and have the properties `:endTime` and `:stream` as explained in Section 5.3. Furthermore, applications may use the optional properties like `:location`. However, most applications need to use domain-specific properties in

[8]TopBraid Composer: http://www.topquadrant.com

events which go beyond the generic temporal and spatial properties introduced above. There are two options on how to implement events with further properties: (i) specialised subclasses of "Event" may be created and instantiated or (ii) the base class may be directly instantiated and domain-specific properties be used in an ad-hoc fashion without a schema other than the base class.

Thus, domain-specific events may have their own schema but alternatively the SDK may also be used for ad-hoc instances extending only the base class. Common to both cases is the minimum requirement of instantiating at least the base class. We go into the details of both cases as follows.

The advantage of creating schemas for domain-specific events is type safety and better support in Java. The downside of the approach is the added effort in creating the schema and that a re-compilation of the Java application is needed as we will see below.

The advantage of not having a schema is that event types can be created and instantiated in an ad-hoc fashion. No re-compilation is required and no effort must be put in the creation of an RDFS schema. The downside is decreased type safety. While the datatypes for the generic event properties such as timestamp and location can be checked, there is no schema to check the types of values supplied to any ad-hoc properties.

In conclusion, the schema-oriented approach is more useful when many event instances of a class will be produced and the effort of creating a schema is negligible. The schema-less approach (where only the base schema is enforced) is more useful for ad-hoc implementations without the overhead of modelling a domain-specific schema or when events must be modelled dynamically without re-compiling an application.

For the schema-oriented approach we use the tool RDFReactor[9] [Völkel 2006] to create Java classes for event models. RDFReactor consumes RDFS schemas for "Event" and its subclasses. Using a template engine Java files are created which must be compiled. The template engine adds all getters and setters for event properties and maps RDF inheritance. The process of

[9]RDFReactor: http://semanticweb.org/wiki/RDFReactor

building the templates can be well integrated in an overall build process by using Maven.

Creating Java classes enables programmers to use a familiar object-oriented abstraction instead of RDF triples. Instantiating an event can be achieved simply by constructing the Java object and calling setters for the event properties. See Listing 5.2 on how to create the example event from Listing 5.1 in Java. The resulting Java object is backed by an RDF model which can be serialised at any moment for any RDF-compliant system like triple stores or our event-based infrastructure introduced in Chapter 7.

```
1  String eventId = EventHelpers.createRandomEventId();
2  Calendar time = Calendar.getInstance();
3
4  FacebookStatusFeedEvent event = new FacebookStatusFeedEvent(
5      EventHelpers.createEmptyModel(eventId),
6      eventId + EVENT_ID_SUFFIX,
7      true);
8  event.setEndTime(time);
9  event.setStream(new URIImpl(Stream.FacebookStatusFeed.getUri()));
10 event.setStatus("I bought some JEANS this morning");
11 event.setFacebookId("100000058455726");
12 event.setFacebookLink(new URIImpl("http://graph.facebook.com/roland.
       stuehmer#"));
13 event.setFacebookLocation("Karlsruhe, Germany");
14 event.setFacebookName("Roland Stühmer");
```

Listing 5.2: Instantiating an Event with predefined Schema (Java)

On line 4 of Listing 5.2 the domain-specific event class is instantiated. The backing RDF model is supplied as one of the parameters. Line 8 ff. shows how domain-specific setters are called subsequently on the event class. Using setters like `setFacebookId` on line 11 the underlying RDF properties and their URIs (e.g. `http://graph.facebook.com/schema/user#id` from the event in Listing 5.1) do not need to be known by a programmer using the SDK.

The schema-less approach on the other hand relies only on the schema of the base class "Event". No compilation of further schemas is required. However, more understanding of RDF is required from the programmer compared to the approach describe above. The schema-less approach consists of just one Java class "Event" with some type-safe setters for the generic event properties from Section 5.3 and some non-type-safe setters for arbitrary ad-hoc properties. Using this approach programmers can quickly instantiate events without having created a schema beforehand and programmatically use arbitrary event properties without re-compiling any SDK classes from templates.

```
1 String eventId = EventHelpers.createRandomEventId();
2 Calendar time = Calendar.getInstance();
3 // Define a namespace for some ad-hoc properties
4 final String USER = "http://graph.facebook.com/schema/user#";
5
6 Event event2 = EventHelpers.builder(eventId)
7     .type(FacebookStatusFeedEvent.RDFS_CLASS)
8     .endTime(time)
9     .stream(Stream.FacebookStatusFeed)
10    .addProperty("http://events...org/types/status", "I bought some
         JEANS this morning")
11    .addProperty(USER + "id", "100000058455726")
12    .addProperty(USER + "link", new URIImpl("http://graph.facebook.com/
         roland.stuehmer#"))
13    .addProperty(USER + "location", "Karlsruhe, Germany")
14    .addProperty(USER + "name", "Roland Stühmer")
15    .build();
```

Listing 5.3: Instantiating an Event with ad-hoc Schema (Java)

Listing 5.3 shows how to create the same example from Listing 5.1 without using a predefined schema. Some type-safe setters are used for basic event properties like `endTime()` on line 8. Non-type-safe setters are shown on line 10 ff. where programmers must specify URIs for properties. The URIs are coined in an ad-hoc fashion by concatenating strings using namespaces as shown, e.g. on line 4. The listing shows how the SDK uses a fluent interface[10] invoking each setter on the result of the previous setter and finally calling the `build()` method. According to the builder pattern[11] first a preliminary builder object is instantiated. The setters of the builder object may be called in any order and pass on the preliminary object. Finally, the `build()` method instantiates the actual Event object. Introducing such a two-phase creation has the advantage of validating the final event object.

[10]Fluent Interface: http://martinfowler.com/bliki/FluentInterface.html
[11]Design Patterns: http://c2.com/cgi/wiki?GangOfFour

This concludes the description of our SDK. It is applied in our scenarios and various implementations of event adapters described in Section 7.6 below.

5.5. Discussion

We now give an overview of the fulfilment of requirements for the event model. At first we list the schemas which were re-used fulfilling Requirement R5: *Ontology re-use*, after that we discuss the remaining requirements.

5.5.1. Schema Re-Use

In order to make our event model as interoperable as possible we re-used existing schemas. The value of interoperability through common ontologies [Pinto and Martins 2000] was discussed in Section 2.1. The following list shows all re-used schemas for the event model and for access control which is used later.

- Time Schemas
  - DOLCE defines Endurant and Occurrent [Gangemi et al. 2002]
  - Properties used: `startTime`, `endTime`
- Location Schemas
  - W3C Geo predicates [Brickley 2003]
  - Class used: `Point`
- Access Control Schemas
  - W3C WebAccessControl [Berners-Lee 2009]
  - Classes used: `Agent` (Users, Groups, Classes), `Mode` (Read, Write)
- Domain Schemas
  - Facebook [Weaver and Tarjan 2012], SIOC [Berrueta 2010]
  - Properties used: e.g. `sioc:content`, `user:link`
  - W3C SSN Ontology[12]
  - Classes used: `Observation`, `Sensor`,

[12] http://www.w3.org/2005/Incubator/ssn/ssnx/ssn

Table 5.1.: Overview of Requirements for the Event Model

Requirement	Fulfilled by: Use of RDF	Fulfilled by: Our Modelling
R1: *Events are first-class objects*		✓
R2: *Time properties*		✓
R3: *Type hierarchy*	✓	✓
R4: *Inter-event relationships*		✓
R5: *Ontology re-use*		✓
R7: *Linked Data Principles for Modelling*	✓	✓
R13: *Open Standards*	✓	
R15: *Adaptivity*	✓	
R16: *Event Metadata*	✓	
R19: *Mobility*		✓

5.5.2. Fulfilment of Requirements

Table 5.1 summarises the coverage of requirements from Chapter 2 by the design decisions made above. The table distinguishes only two main design decisions for the sake of simplicity. The first is the use of RDF (second column from the right). When mapping the fulfilment of requirements, this decision subsumes many facets of RDF, e.g. being a standard by the W3C, supporting hierarchies of classes through RDFS, its use for Linked Data on the Web and its versatility of mixing schemas. The second design decision subsumes our modelling decisions, i.e. how we use RDF (rightmost column). The modelling subsumes decisions which we made with respect to the event properties we use, the properties we re-use and the URIs we coined.

Table 5.1 can be understood line by line: The requirement *Events are first-class objects* is fulfilled by our modelling. The same is true for *Time properties*. The requirement for a *Type hierarchy* is supported both by RDF but also by our modelling in the way we designed the hierarchy of events for our scenarios. *Inter-event relationships* are supported by our modelling in that we designed the necessary event properties. *Ontology re-use* is supported by our choice of pre-existing schemas wherever possible. *Linked Data Principles for Modelling* are made possible by the use of RDF, a necessary precondition for Linked Data, as well as by our modelling which favours dereferenceable URIs. The use of *Open Standards* is fulfilled by our decision to use RDF. The same holds true for *Adaptivity* which is supported by the flexibility of using, mixing and evolving RDF schemas. *Event Metadata* is supported by the use of RDF as a data and metadata modelling language. Finally, *Mobility* is supported by our modelling using W3C standards for location tagging.

This concludes the design of the event model. In Chapter 6 below we explain the event pattern language which facilitates processing of events based on the model in real-time. Further below in Chapter 7 we describe the infrastructure used to organise, subscribe, and process events using the format and the pattern language.

6 A Pattern Language for Events

To combine real-time data and historic data we propose a language called Big Data Processing Language (BDPL). The language is designed to be used in a distributed setting of RDF streams and RDF static data.

6.1. Introduction: A real-time Query Language for RDF Event Streams

Our language is based on ETALIS, previous work in event processing. ETALIS is an event processing system, with an accompanied event pattern language, cf. [Aničić 2012, Part II]. The system is based on logic programming. Complex events are *deduced* from simpler events by means of applying event patterns. Event patterns are defined as *deductive rules*, and events including their attributes are represented as sets of *facts*. Every time a simple event (relevant w.r.t. the set of monitored complex events) occurs, the system updates its knowledge base, i.e. it adds respective facts to the internal state of complex events. Essentially, this internal state encodes what atomic events have already happened and what events are still missing for the completion of a certain complex event. Complex events are detected and propagated as soon as the last event required for their detection has occurred. This is an important difference from query-driven approaches to logic programming where polling is required to produce results. Knowledge about which occurrence of an event furthers the detection of complex events (including the relationships between complex events and events they consist of) are given by deductive rules. ETALIS defines an expressive complex event description language with a rule-based syntax and a declarative, formal semantics. The language is founded on an execution model that compiles complex event patterns into logic rules and enables timely, event-driven detection of complex events. New rules can efficiently re-use common subexpressions of existing rules and rules can be added and removed from the query execution graph at runtime.

Our language, BDPL, is a language executed on top of ETALIS as a front-end language compiled to ETALIS rules. The purpose of BDPL is to fulfil the requirements of RDF events which are discussed in Chapter 2. For this thesis we go beyond the related work to deal with structured events consisting of many RDF triples as opposed to one triple per event. This greatly increases the ease-of-use of our implementation in environments where events have many attributes as opposed to a single triple per event (cf. the discussion in Section 4.1). In other words, BDPL works with structured events which can combine many properties, whereas previous designs only looked at one triple at a time. An event is thus now a graph whereas it used to be a triple before. This is much closer to real-world systems which must understand events with multiple facets.

As part of allowing for multiple attributes, the timestamps in each event are now made explicit (as another event property) whereas they were merely second-class citizens in related work being added in the background to each tuple. This allows our system to transmit the time as part of the event. Using time in events enables the support of "application time". This means that a source specifies the occurrence time of an event as opposed to "system time" where the receiving system specifies the time.

Our language supports hybrid queries mixing real-time event processing with historic data. Events which are processed in real-time often do not contain all context which is needed to process them in a meaningful way. Also, longer-term data analysis must operate on archived streams [Dindar et al. 2011]. For these reasons a current, real-time view of events is not enough. Therefore, our language combines efficient, incremental real-time monitoring of events with historic queries in one hybrid language. Architectures supporting such languages are called Lambda Architectures in [Marz and Warren 2015]. Lambda Architectures support real-time data and historic data in specialised systems but with one homogeneous query language, see Section 4.4.

6.2. Requirements

The event pattern language must fulfil certain requirements. These were collected in Chapter 2. In the following we briefly reiterate the requirements specific to the language.

Requirement R9: *Support for the data model* must be fulfilled by the language to be used with the data model of events in RDF. R10: *Hybrid Querying* requires the language to support queries mixing in-memory, real-time matching of events with federated querying of historic data. Temporal operators must be supported by the real-time matching to address R11: *Temporal Operators*. Moreover, R13: *Open Standards* must be observed. Furthermore, R14: *Event-driven* requires the language to support event-driven applications by offering fine-grained event-at-a-time operators which can be used to selectively react to interesting situations. R15: *Adaptivity* must be supported to enable multi-user systems with changing demands for varying situations of interest and for evolving schemas. Finally, R18: *Query Expressivity* subsumes the compliance of our language with the needs from the scenarios.

6.3. Formalism: Syntax and Semantics of the Language

We modelled BDPL close to SPARQL 1.1 but with focus on integrating primitives from event processing. We describe our design in detail as follows.

From the SPARQL 1.1 language we use the following subset: CONSTRUCT queries without operators UNION and subqueries, OPTIONAL or LIMIT clauses. UNION and subqueries are omitted for simplicity of our implementation; they can be emulated by issuing several separate queries. LIMIT on the other hand is not applicable in real-time queries because queries are expected to return an unbounded set of results until the queries are unregistered. So LIMIT was omitted. We introduced window operators instead to group events into finite sets without limiting the number of results overall. OPTIONAL is omitted but is a useful enhancement for future versions.

We syntactically extend this subset of SPARQL in two ways: (i) with primitives from event processing such as time windows [Aničić 2012, Chapter 6] to enable temporal processing and (ii) to distinguish real-time data from historic data.

Introducing temporal processing operators is needed to match events in certain relationships such as sequences and time windows. Also, temporal operators may be overloaded to deal with both interval-based and point-based events as discussed for Requirement R11: *Temporal Operators* in Chapter 2.

Distinguishing real-time data from historic data is done using the syntax `EVENT` and `GRAPH`. The distinction is needed to facilitate federation of queries. Bound variables may be used to join events based on their payloads with historic data. Variables may be bound anywhere in the WHERE clause: in the individual event instances and in historic data. To match the entire query a suitable binding must be found for all occurrences of each variable or otherwise the event can be discarded. Section 7.2.3 explains the joins of federated data in detail.

We introduce the formal grammar for BDPL in Backus-Naur Form (BNF). The full text of the grammar is available as open-source software, cf. Appendix A.3.

The first part of the grammar defines the syntax of BDPL as CONSTRUCT queries like in SPARQL. The two remaining query types in SPARQL, namely ASK and SELECT queries, are not applicable to event processing. ASK queries only return Boolean results which is not expressive enough to model derived events. SELECT queries return arbitrary-length tuples which is not appropriate to model triples for derived events. CONSTRUCT queries are the only query form providing an RDF to RDF mapping[1].

⟨*ConstructQuery*⟩ ::= '`CONSTRUCT`' (⟨*ConstructTemplate*⟩
⟨*BdplWhereClause*⟩ ⟨*SolutionModifier*⟩)

⟨*ConstructTemplate*⟩ ::= ⟨*LBRACE*⟩ ⟨*TriplesBlock*⟩ ⟨*RBRACE*⟩

⟨*BdplWhereClause*⟩ ::= ('`WHERE`')? ⟨*LBRACE*⟩
⟨*RealTimeEventQuery*⟩ ⟨*HistoricalEventQuery*⟩
⟨*RBRACE*⟩

⟨*SolutionModifier*⟩ ::= (⟨*HavingClause*⟩)?

The previous snippet shows the initial productions of the grammar in BNF. The `ConstructQuery` exhibits standard SPARQL syntax except for the modified WHERE clause. We introduce the most important features of BDPL there. Thus, the so-called `BdplWhereClause` consists of a real-time part and a historic part. The latter contains unmodified SPARQL whereas the `RealTimeEventQuery` contains our new keyword `EVENT` along with temporal operators needed for event processing. The real-time part is explained in detail as follows.

⟨*RealTimeEventQuery*⟩ ::= ⟨*WindowClause*⟩ | (⟨*EventPattern*⟩)

⟨*WindowClause*⟩ ::= ⟨*WINDOW*⟩ ⟨*LBRACE*⟩ ⟨*EventPattern*⟩ ⟨*RBRACE*⟩
⟨*WindowDecl*⟩ (⟨*FilterOrBind*⟩)*

[1] Although the other query forms are not applicable to the design of BDPL, they nevertheless are used in this work for other purposes: SELECT queries are employed in Section 7.2 to integrate historic RDF backends and ASK queries in Section 7.3 to evaluate RDF access control.

⟨*EventPattern*⟩ ::= ⟨*EventClause*⟩ (⟨*BdplBinOperators*⟩ ⟨*EventClause*⟩)*
| ⟨*NotClause*⟩
| ⟨*TimeBasedEvent*⟩
| (⟨*LBRACE*⟩ ⟨*EventPattern*⟩ ⟨*RBRACE*⟩)

⟨*EventClause*⟩ ::= 'EVENT' ⟨*VarOrIRIref*⟩ ⟨*LBRACE*⟩ ⟨*EventGraphPattern*⟩ ⟨*RBRACE*⟩

⟨*BdplBinOperators*⟩ ::= ⟨*SEQ*⟩ | ⟨*AND*⟩ | ⟨*OR*⟩ | ⟨*EQUALS*⟩ | ⟨*OPTIONALSEQ*⟩ | ⟨*EQUALSOPTIONAL*⟩

⟨*NotClause*⟩ ::= 'NOT' ⟨*LBRACE*⟩ (⟨*EventClause*⟩ | ⟨*TimeBasedEvent*⟩)
(⟨*EventClause*⟩ | ⟨*TimeBasedEvent*⟩)
(⟨*EventClause*⟩ | ⟨*TimeBasedEvent*⟩) ⟨*RBRACE*⟩

⟨*EventGraphPattern*⟩ ::= (⟨*TriplesBlock*⟩)? (⟨*Filter*⟩ (⟨*DOT*⟩)? (⟨*TriplesBlock*⟩)?)*

⟨*HistoricalEventQuery*⟩ ::= (⟨*GraphGraphPattern*⟩)*

The previous snippet shows the details of the real-time part. The `EventClause` marks a pattern to match one event. It starts with the keyword `EVENT`. The clause can be composed into patterns of multiple events using operators or windows. The `NotClause` is a special operator which is ternary. Its syntax `NOT {A, B, C}` is matched if an event of type B does not occur within A and C.

The `WindowClause` declares window operators of different types. A window operator groups events from an unbounded stream into sequential finite sets of events, called windows [Etzion and Niblett 2010]. A time-based window is set of events happening in a certain time-interval, e.g. within the last five minutes. A count-based window is a set of events defined by the order of events, e.g. the last five events. Both types of windows are supported including the specification of the window length.

The `HistoricalEventQuery` at the end of the snippet is the syntax for the historical part of the query. It consists of standard patterns from SPARQL.

Listing 6.1 shows an example query in BDPL. The purpose of this query is to notify the recipient whenever three users of the social network Facebook report something of interest in their status message. In this case the query matches the word "JEANS" in their status message during a time window of thirty minutes. The real-time data is combined with historic data from past tweets of one of the friends.

The example demonstrates several facts about our query language:

1. We modelled BDPL as close to SPARQL 1.1 [Harris and Seaborne 2010] as possible. Exceptions are being made for necessary event operators and the denotations of events compared to non-event historic data.
2. Event derivation (the modelling of the resulting complex event) is handled through a CONSTRUCT clause as in SPARQL 1.1. The clause (starting on line 6) contains a template of triples for the complex event. Additional attributes like the timestamps are handled implicitly. They are derived automatically from the participating simple events which form the complex event according to the semantics of the event operators.
3. The event pattern is modelled in the subsequent WHERE clause starting on line 12.
4. The pattern contains several events combined with event operators (e.g. SEQ on line 21) nested in a sliding time window defined by the `xsd:duration` on line 37. The matching semantics of the event operators is described by [Aničić 2012, Chapter 7] in terms of the event's time stamps along with an execution model of the language.
5. Each event is matched according to its content in addition to the temporal matching described before. Matching of event content is done similarly to the GRAPH clause in SPARQL 1.1. The clause, however, is denoted with EVENT here (e.g. on line 14) to distinguish the real-time parts of the query from the optional historic parts. The historic parts are evaluated after the real-time part is detected. The syntax for historic data uses standard GRAPH clauses from SPARQL 1.1. (Cf. line 39.)
6. Bound variables may be used to join events with each other and with historic data. The variable `?friend3` is an example. It is bound in the third event on line 34 and in the historic part of the query on line 42. To match the query a suitable binding must be found

```
PREFIX rdf:    <http://www.w3.org/1999/02/22-rdf-syntax-ns#>
PREFIX user:   <http://graph.facebook.com/schema/user#>
PREFIX sioc:   <http://rdfs.org/sioc/ns#>
PREFIX :       <http://events.event-processing.org/types/>

CONSTRUCT {
  :e rdf:type :FacebookCepResult .
  :e :stream <http://streams...org/ids/FacebookCepResults#stream> .
  :e user:name ?friend1 , ?friend2 , ?friend3 .
  :e :status ?status1 , ?status2 , ?status3 , ?historicTweet .
}
WHERE {
  WINDOW {
    EVENT ?id1 {
      ?e1 rdf:type :FacebookStatusFeedEvent .
      ?e1 :stream <http://streams.../FacebookStatusFeed#stream> .
      ?e1 :status ?status1 .
      ?e1 user:name ?friend1 .
      FILTER contains(?status1, "JEANS")
      }
    SEQ
    EVENT ?id2 {
      ?e2 rdf:type :FacebookStatusFeedEvent .
      ?e2 :stream <http://streams.../FacebookStatusFeed#stream> .
      ?e2 :status ?status2 .
      ?e2 user:name ?friend2 .
      FILTER contains(?status2, "JEANS")
      }
    SEQ
    EVENT ?id3 {
      ?e3 rdf:type :FacebookStatusFeedEvent .
      ?e3 :stream <http://streams.../FacebookStatusFeed#stream> .
      ?e3 :status ?status3 .
      ?e3 user:name ?friend3 .
      FILTER contains(?status3, "JEANS")
      }
  } ("PT30M"^^xsd:duration, sliding)

  GRAPH ?id4 {
    ?e4 rdf:type :TwitterEvent .
    ?e4 :stream <http://streams.../TwitterFeed#stream> .
    ?e4 :screenName ?friend3 .
    ?e4 sioc:content ?historicTweet .
    }
}
```

Listing 6.1: BDPL Query Example

for all occurrences of each variable or otherwise the event can be discarded.

7. We extended the underlying engine ETALIS to execute XPath functions such as `contains()` to be more expressive with regard to handling XML data types. (Cf. line 19.)

This concludes the specification of BDPL, our design for matching structured, rich events in RDF. Section 6.4 describes how BDPL is compiled into rules which are understood by the underlying execution engine ETALIS.

6.4. Query Decomposition

A BDPL query consists of a real-time part and a historic part. A new query is parsed using our grammar. From the resulting parse tree two kinds of code are generated: (i) the real-time part which is transformed into rules for the underlying event processing engine ETALIS and (ii) the historic part which is transformed into one or more SPARQL queries for distributed storage backends. We explain the real-time part in the following, whereas we explain the historic part in Section 7.2.

The real-time part of BDPL is compiled into ETALIS Language for Events (ELE) rules [Aničić 2012, Part II]. They are understood by ETALIS. Listing 6.2 shows ELE code generated from the query in Listing 6.1. Since ELE does not handle events in RDF we extended it with Prolog rules to do so.

The first part of the ELE rule in Listing 6.2 (before the arrow "<-" on line 42) is the left hand side of the rule. The derived event is constructed there. This is generated from the CONSTRUCT clause in the original BDPL query. Each predicate `generateConstructResult()` creates another triple or set of triples in the derived event.

```
1 r1 'rule:' complex(CEID)
2 do (
3     generateConstructResult(
4         ['http://events.event-processing.org/types/e'],
5         ['http://www.w3.org/1999/02/22-rdf-syntax-ns#type'],
6         ['http://events.event-processing.org/types/FacebookCepResult'],
7         CEID),
```

```
    generateConstructResult(
        ['http://events.event-processing.org/types/e'],
        ['http://graph.facebook.com/schema/user#name'],
        [FRIEND1],
        CEID),
    generateConstructResult(
        ['http://events.event-processing.org/types/e'],
        ['http://graph.facebook.com/schema/user#name'],
        [FRIEND2],
        CEID),
    generateConstructResult(
        ['http://events.event-processing.org/types/e'],
        ['http://graph.facebook.com/schema/user#name'],
        [FRIEND3],
        CEID),
    generateConstructResult(
        ['http://events.event-processing.org/types/e'],
        ['http://events.event-processing.org/types/discussionTopic'],
        [ABOUT1],
        CEID),
    generateConstructResult(
        ['http://events.event-processing.org/types/e'],
        ['http://events.event-processing.org/types/discussionTopic'],
        [ABOUT2],
        CEID),
    generateConstructResult(
        ['http://events.event-processing.org/types/e'],
        ['http://events.event-processing.org/types/discussionTopic'],
        [ABOUT3],
        CEID),
    decrementReferenceCounter(ID1), collectGarbage(ID1),
    decrementReferenceCounter(ID2), collectGarbage(ID2),
    decrementReferenceCounter(ID3), collectGarbage(ID3)
)
<-
('http://events.event-processing.org/types/FacebookStatusFeedEvent'(ID1
    )
  'WHERE' (
    (rdf(E1, 'http://www.w3.org/1999/02/22-rdf-syntax-ns#type',
      'http://events.event-processing.org/types/FacebookStatusFeedEvent
          ', ID1)),
    (rdf(E1, 'http://events.event-processing.org/types/status', ABOUT1,
        ID1)),
    (rdf(E1, 'http://events.event-processing.org/types/name', FRIEND1,
        ID1)),
    (xpath(element(sparqlFilter, [keyWord=ABOUT1], []),
      //sparqlFilter(contains(@keyWord,'JEANS')), _)),
    incrementReferenceCounter(ID1)
  )
 ) 'SEQ'
 ('http://events.event-processing.org/types/FacebookStatusFeedEvent'(
      ID2)
  'WHERE' (
```

```
56        (rdf(E2, 'http://www.w3.org/1999/02/22-rdf-syntax-ns#type',
57          'http://events.event-processing.org/types/FacebookStatusFeedEvent
              ',
58          ID2)),
59        (rdf(E2, 'http://events.event-processing.org/types/status',
60          ABOUT2, ID2)),
61        (rdf(E2, 'http://events.event-processing.org/types/name',
62          FRIEND2, ID2)),
63        (xpath(element(sparqlFilter, [keyWord=ABOUT2], []),
64          //sparqlFilter(contains(@keyWord,'JEANS')), _)),
65        incrementReferenceCounter(ID2)
66    )
67  ) 'SEQ'
68  ('http://events.event-processing.org/types/FacebookStatusFeedEvent'(
        ID3)
69    'WHERE' (
70        (rdf(E3, 'http://www.w3.org/1999/02/22-rdf-syntax-ns#type',
71          'http://events.event-processing.org/types/FacebookStatusFeedEvent
              ',
72          ID3)),
73        (rdf(E3, 'http://events.event-processing.org/types/status',
74          ABOUT3, ID3)),
75        (rdf(E3, 'http://events.event-processing.org/types/name',
76          FRIEND3, ID3)),
77        (xpath(element(sparqlFilter, [keyWord=ABOUT3], []),
78          //sparqlFilter(contains(@keyWord,'JEANS')), _)),
79        incrementReferenceCounter(ID3),
80        random(1000000, 9000000, CEID)
81    )
82  ).
83  event_rule_property(r1,event_rule_window,1800).
```

Listing 6.2: Output of BDPL Parser (ETALIS ELE Syntax)

The predicates `decrementReferenceCounter()` and `collectGarbage()` deal with the garbage collection of the participating simple events. According to the number of rules registered in the system a simple event may be consumed several times before it can be collected. The corresponding Prolog predicates maintain the usage counters and execute the collection of garbage.

The remainder of the query (line 43 ff.) deals with the right hand side of the rule, defining the constraints on the simple events. This is generated from the WHERE clause in the original BDPL query. The temporal operator `SEQ` from ETALIS can be seen in the example. The constraint from the time window in BDPL is sent to ETALIS separately (line 83) as a rule property containing the window length in seconds.

The predicate `rdf()` is used to match RDF quadruples in simple events (line 45 ff.). The predicate `xpath()` is used to apply several useful XPath functions to increase the expressivity in matching events (e.g. line 49). The predicate `random()` is used to create new event IDs for the derived event (line 80).

We use the following Prolog libraries to execute BDPL:

- library(semweb/rdf_db)[2] to handle RDF triples
- library(xpath)[3] to implement XPath functions
- library(random)[4] to provide new, random IDs for derived events

This concludes the description of our language BDPL and its transformation for the underlying event processing engine.

6.5. Discussion

Table 6.1 summarises the coverage of requirements specific to the pattern language from Chapter 2. The table distinguishes two main design decisions for the sake of simplicity: The first is the use of SPARQL (second column from the right). When mapping the fulfilment of requirements, this decision subsumes many facets of SPARQL, e.g. being a standard by the W3C, being tailored specifically for processing RDF or its expressiveness when matching graph data. The second design decision subsumes the extensions to SPARQL we made (rightmost column). These extensions include e.g. the temporal operators, event-at-a-time semantics and hybrid querying we added when designing BDPL.

Table 6.1 can be understood line by line as follows: The requirement *Support for the data model* is fulfilled by the use of SPARQL in our work. On the other hand, *Hybrid Querying* is fulfilled not by basic SPARQL but by the extensions we make to it. Likewise, *Temporal Operators* are supported by

[2] **semweb/rdf_db:** The RDF database: http://www.swi-prolog.org/pldoc/man?section=semweb-rdf-db

[3] **xpath:** Select nodes in an XML DOM: http://www.swi-prolog.org/pldoc/man?section=xpath

[4] **random:** Random numbers: http://www.swi-prolog.org/pldoc/man?section=random

Table 6.1.: Overview of Requirements for the Pattern Language

Requirement	Fulfilled by: Use of SPARQL	Fulfilled by: Our Extensions
R9: *Support for the data model*	✓	
R10: *Hybrid Querying*		✓
R11: *Temporal Operators*		✓
R13: *Open Standards*	✓(1)	
R14: *Event-driven*		✓
R15: *Adaptivity*	✓	✓
R18: *Query Expressivity*	✓	✓

our extensions. The requirement for *Open Standards* is fulfilled by basing our approach on SPARQL but with the limitation (cf. (1) in Table 6.1) of making extensions, i.e. changes to the standard. The requirement of being *Event-driven* is fulfilled by our extensions by adding event processing operators to the language. *Adaptivity* is supported by making any two queries isolated from each other. Thus, adding an event pattern never steals events from another pattern. For standard SPARQL CONSTRUCT queries this is a given and for our extensions we ascertain that all queries consume events in isolation. Finally, the required *Query Expressivity* for our scenarios is supported both by basic SPARQL and by our extensions; cf. [Benaben et al. 2013].

7

An Infrastructure for Events

This chapter describes the software artefacts which were designed as part of this thesis to answer the research questions. The artefacts are part of a larger system architecture for Web-oriented event processing. The architecture not only includes event processing as part of this work but also access control for streaming data as well as storage and a service bus which are contributed by third parties mentioned below.

7.1. Architecture

There are two main layers in our conceptual architecture; event processing and storage: The storage layer provides a publish/subscribe mechanism allowing storing and retrieving events. Storage is organised into partitions to allow federated queries. The second layer is event processing. It enables the deduction of events from low level events based on event patterns. The full picture is presented in Figure 7.1.

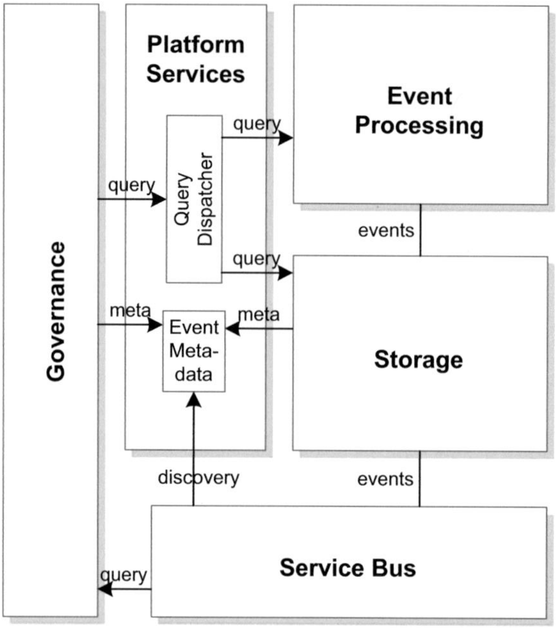

Figure 7.1.: Architecture of the System (Block Diagram)

7.1.1. Components

The system architecture as presented in Figure 7.1 is comprised of the following components:

- The **Service Bus** provides the Service-oriented architecture (SOA) and Event-driven architecture (EDA) infrastructure for components and end user services.
- The **Governance** component enables users to specify permissions on streams. Permissions are enforced on incoming queries.

- The **Storage** component provides storage of events and historic data as well as forwarding of events [Filali et al. 2011].
- The **Event Processing** component has the role of detecting complex events and reasoning over events. It contains the main contributions of this work.
- The **Platform Services** incorporate several functional additions to the platform as a whole: Query Dispatcher has the role of decomposing and deploying BDPL queries. The Event Metadata component stores information about events and streams to facilitate search.

The **service bus** (at bottom of Figure 7.1) is an event-oriented middleware. It is contributed by a third party, see also Appendix A.1 on open-source artefacts. The service bus supports publish/subscribe interaction based on event topics. Its purpose is the standards-based integration of event users: producers and consumers.

The next element in the stack is **storage** (on the right of Figure 7.1). Its purpose is to store events for non-real-time (e.g. analytical) queries along with other static data. Storage is implemented as a distributed quadruple store to organise event's triples according to their provenance: Apart from the organization in graphs, events are furthermore organised in streams. The stream representing a topic on the service bus is specified in each event. The streams are used for partitioning the storage onto several nodes. For the storage nodes we use interchangeable implementations of Virtuoso[1], 4store[2] and EventCloud[3]. Subsequently, queries are federated accordingly by evaluating the stream property in each pattern.

Events are relayed immediately to **event processing** which is the next element on the stack (top right of Figure 7.1). Its purpose is to match real-time queries against streaming events on-line and to orchestrate any historic parts of the queries with the nodes of the storage component.

[1]Virtuoso Open Source: http://virtuoso.openlinksw.com/

[2]4store, RDF database: http://4store.org/

[3]EventCloud was used in our evaluation in Section 8.4

7.1.2. Communication

Communication inside the platform as well as with external components relies on three main protocols for specific purposes. The protocols are ProActive[4] (based on RMI[5]), SOAP (using WS-Notification messages) and REST.

ProActive: Internally and among each other the components communicate using ProActive based on RMI. ProActive is a component model and a distributed middleware. It realises remote communication between distributed components by translating method calls to RMI. Components may be linked and unlinked dynamically according to their interfaces. ProActive provides good type safety, being implemented in pure Java. We chose ProActive because it is the only component model suitable for distributed deployment unlike, e.g. OSGI, and because it is a framework which allows dynamic changes to a distributed topology, e.g. unlike Apache Storm.

SOAP: The service bus communicates with external components (event producers and consumers) through SOAP using WS-Notification messages. Thus, event publishing and subscription is standardised by WS-Notification[6]. The specification defines the schemas of Notify, Subscribe and Unsubscribe messages. Subsequently, the event schema contributed by this work (cf. Chapter 5) is then embedded inside Notify message envelopes. Each event is associated with a topic and subscriptions are based on such topics. We selected WS-Notification because of its platform independence and because it is an official standard for topic-based publish/ subscribe (for publish/subscribe see Section 3.5).

REST: The platform additionally exposes its external APIs using representational state transfer (REST). These APIs for publish/subscribe offer a

[4]ProActive Parallel Suite: http://proactive.activeeon.com
[5]Java Remote Method Invocation, the object-oriented equivalent of remote procedure calls
[6]WS-Notification: https://www.oasis-open.org/committees/wsn/

simpler message format; however, the schemas are not standardised like WS-Notification. We implemented the REST APIs to obtain simple access for ad-hoc clients such as JavaScript-based management clients of our platform. A JavaScript-based pattern manager using REST is described in Section 7.4.

In conclusion, RMI-communication is used to connect our components internally, SOAP-communication is used with external components where standardised protocols are available such as WS-Notification and finally REST-communication is used externally where no standards previously existed.

7.2. Event Processing

Hereinafter we focus on the component **event processing** introduced in Section 7.1. Its implementation is referred to as Distributed Complex Event Processing (DCEP). To connect with the remainder of the platform DCEP has inputs and outputs, defined by interfaces.

7.2.1. Interfaces

DCEP *provides* two interfaces (on the left edge of Figure 7.2), the `DcepMonitoringApi` and the `DcepManagementApi`. They are used by the external governance component to manage the registered event patterns and to configure monitoring.

DCEP *consumes* three interfaces (on the right edge of Figure 7.2), the `PublishApi`, the `SubscribeApi` and the `PutGetApi`. They are used to access external components in the platform to subscribe to necessary simple events needed to fulfil patterns, to publish complex events and to fetch historic data from storage.

7.2.2. Components

Internally, DCEP is divided into subcomponents which are designed for a distributed deployment (cf. Figure 7.2). The figure shows the components `DistributedEtalis`, `QueryDispatcher` and `DcepManager` contained in the global component `Dcep`.

`DistributedEtalis` implements the core event processing logic in Java and Prolog. It can be instantiated and deployed multiple times. The remaining components are singletons: `Dcep` contains all other components and exposes external APIs to other parts of the overall system such as storage and the service bus. `DcepManager` holds the logic for monitoring `DistributedEtalis`. Finally, `QueryDispatcher` holds the BDPL parser separating real-time and historic parts of a query.

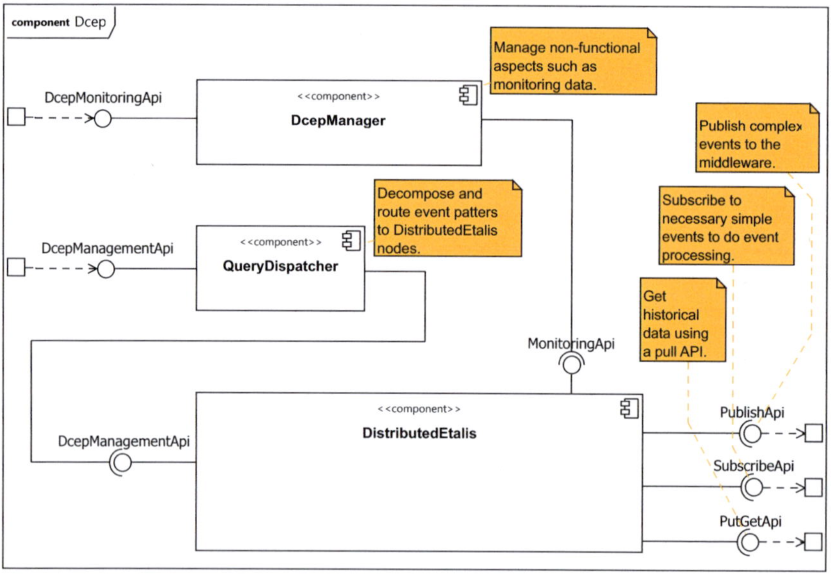

Figure 7.2.: Subcomponents of DCEP (Component Diagram)

7.2.3. Algorithm

Intuitively, a hybrid query is fulfilled if there is a *mapping* (according to the semantics of SPARQL [Pérez et al. 2009]) for all variables from the real-time patterns and a *compatible mapping* for the historic data at the time of the real-time answer. This entails the computation of joins between the data at some point in time. Operationally, real-time patterns are applied to the streams first. This is done in a continuous fashion, listening for matching events. Results are detected incrementally and are produced as soon as the last events arrive to fulfil the part. When such a real-time result is reported, the historical parts of the query are executed. The variable mappings from both the real-time part and the historic parts will be checked for compatibility. The combined result is then created via joins of any bound variables.

After a non-empty result is found, the CONSTRUCT template is filled to create a new event from the result. This event is published as any other event and may be received by users, services and devices. This includes the event participating in further queries to create layered, higher abstractions of further complex events. (Cf. *event abstraction hierarchies* in [Luckham 2001, Section 3.7].)

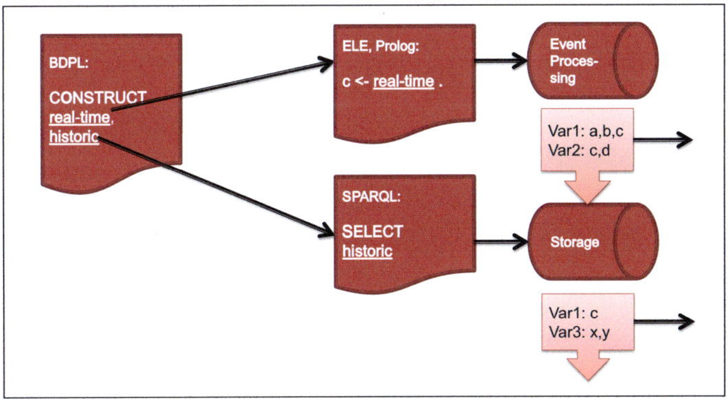

Figure 7.3.: Query Decomposition, Part 1: Calculation of the Results

Figure 7.3 shows how queries are decomposed. A query in Big Data Processing Language (BDPL) consists of a real-time part and a historic part as indicated on the left of the figure. A new query is parsed using our grammar. From the resulting parse tree two kinds of code are generated: (i) the real-time part is transformed into rules for the underlying event processing engine ETALIS and (ii) the historic part is transformed into one or more SPARQL queries for distributed storage backends. The process is indicated in the centre column of the figure.

The nature of Linked Data is exploited during query decomposition. Each pattern in the historical query (cf. `GraphGraphPattern` in the grammar above) defines a stream property. This property links an event to its stream. See Listing 6.1, line 41, for an example linking to a stream of Twitter events.

This information is used with real-time events and historical events. With historical events separate historical queries are created from BDPL for each separate historic stream. Data in our storage system is partitioned by stream. Queries which are decomposed in this way are later fired when it is time to retrieve historic results. Such requests are only made to those backends which have the relevant data according to the partitioning in our system. Additionally, links to streams are used to obtain real-time data. There, data are subscribed to in a topic-based fashion similar to the partitioning of our historic data. Each stream URI can be used to subscribe to the topic containing the streaming data.

The decomposition of a query happens when the query is registered. The real-time part is then registered with our event processing system immediately, cf. top right of Figure 7.3. Whenever the real-time part produces a result, the corresponding historical parts are executed, cf. bottom right of the figure. This happens by executing each separate historical query at its corresponding storage backend. The links in stream descriptions are followed to find the appropriate backend.

The process of answering different parts of a query by different backend systems is called federated querying [Harris and Seaborne 2010] in the terminology of SPARQL. Joins are allowed across the entire query. This means individual results from the backend systems must be joined to produce a final result.

Equi-joins in SPARQL are computed between graph patterns which declare a shared SPARQL variable. In Listing 6.1 the variable `?friend3` is an example which is shared by several graph patterns. To find valid bindings, SPARQL execution engines must compute equi-joins between graph patterns with shared variables. Further types of joins are required by the FILTER clause using non-equi comparators between shared variables.

SPARQL provides support for making joins in federated queries more efficient. In a federated setting intermediate results of a join are transmitted between systems to produce a final result in one place. The size of intermediate results participating in a join must be minimised to reduce (a) the transmission costs and (b) the computational cost of the final join. To that end SPARQL queries can be constrained by variable bindings which restrict the possible results of joins.

If variables are bound in the real-time part of a query, there will be a set of possible values, i.e. bindings, for that variable once the real-time part has a solution (i.e. the event pattern was matched). The resulting intermediate variable bindings are then transmitted to the storage systems along with the historic queries. The historic queries may then be pre-joined with the transmitted data.

Sending intermediate data to the historic storage systems for joining and not vice versa usually optimises the join order. We assume that the real-time parts of our queries usually match a small set of in-memory, time-constrained data. Thus, its intermediate results are usually smaller than the results from historic, archived streams where a lot of data are queried.

Listing 7.1 shows the example of a historic query as it is sent to a storage system including a very small variable binding. The query is statically generated during the decomposition of the BDPL query from the previous example, Listing 6.1. However, before it is sent in the form presented in the listing, the query is amended with variable bindings for the shared variable `?friend3` on line 13. The VALUES clause is a part of standard

```
1 PREFIX rdf:      <http://www.w3.org/1999/02/22-rdf-syntax-ns#>
2 PREFIX sioc:     <http://rdfs.org/sioc/ns#>
3 PREFIX :         <http://events.event-processing.org/types/>
4
5 SELECT ?friend3 ?historicTweet
6 WHERE {
7   GRAPH ?id4 {
8     ?e4 rdf:type :TwitterEvent .
9     ?e4 :stream <http://streams.../TwitterFeed#stream> .
10    ?e4 :screenName ?friend3 .
11    ?e4 sioc:content ?historicTweet .
12    }
13  VALUES ?friend3 { "rolandstuehmer" }
14 }
```

Listing 7.1: Historic Query Example generated from BDPL

SPARQL to support federated queries. The clause may be used to transmit lists of bindings for one or more variables. In the example on line 13 only one binding for the variable was found in the real-time part. It is transmitted as "inline data" [Harris and Seaborne 2010] together with the query. Its purpose is to restrict the fulfilment of the historic part optimizing the final join operation.

Other than the VALUES clause the historic query exhibits the following characteristics:

1. The query uses standard SPARQL 1.1 [Harris and Seaborne 2010]. Thus, our event processing system can be used with any RDF triple stores as the backends.
2. The SELECT query form of SPARQL is used. Cf. line 5 of the listing. Sets of values must be exchanged with the backends. Thus, for intermediate results there is no need to exchange full triples. Full triples, supported only by CONSTRUCT queries, will be created only in our final step when filling the overall BDPL with final join results.
3. The WHERE clause starting on line 6 is extracted unchanged from the originating BDPL query in Listing 6.1.
4. The variables in the projection on line 5 are only those variables shared by this historic query with the rest (i.e. "the outside") of the

BDPL query. It is the task of our code generator to create this set of variables for each historic query when decomposing BDPL.

5. The variables in VALUES on line 13 are only those variables (i) shared with the rest of the query and (ii) having previous bindings from the real-time part. It is the task of our event processing system to populate this set of values at runtime when the real-time part of the query returns results before the historic query is dispatched to its backend.

The query is subsequently dispatched to the corresponding storage backend which holds the archived stream, i.e. partition, `TwitterFeed` as expressed on line 10.

The query may hold more than one GRAPH clause if the originating BDPL query has more than one historic parts matching the `TwitterFeed`. Also, more than one separate historic query may be generated, if there are historic parts matching other streams archived at other backends.

If more than one result set is returned from the storage backends, a final join must be executed for any shared variable. Thus, our system further optimises the join performance by planning the join order for the final join. After counting the size of the intermediate results these results are joined with each other in ascending order from smallest to largest.

Figure 7.4 continues the diagram from the previous figure. Here, the transmission of variable bindings is depicted in the column on the left. The final join for all variables is depicted at centre and top right of the figure.

The bottom right of Figure 7.4 shows how the final values are filled in the CONSTRUCT template to create the derived event. The values accurately fulfil all predicates of the overall query while the query was fulfilled across one or more storage systems and our event processing system in a federated manner. Full triples, i.e. valid RDF, results filling the template.

Algorithm 1 summarises the steps taken to fulfil a hybrid query with both its real-time and its historic parts. The life-cycle defined in the algorithm starts by registering the query and ends by unregistering it. First, a new BDPL query is received from a user (on line 1). Subsequently, the query is

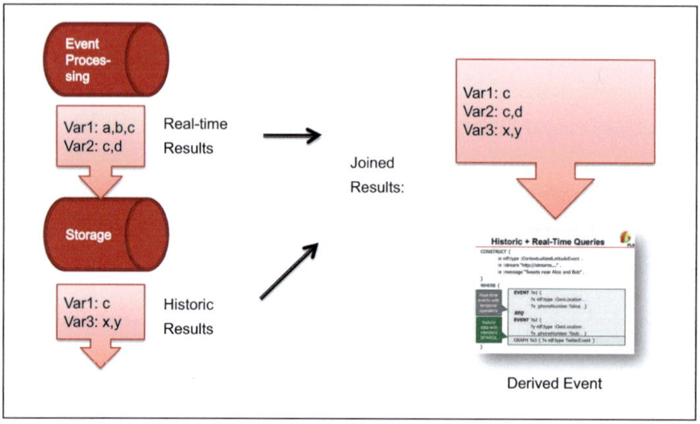

Figure 7.4.: Query Decomposition, Part 2: Join of the Results

decomposed into its real-time part and historic parts. The real-time part is extracted and cross-compiled into the language for ETALIS. The historic parts are extracted as SPARQL. Then the real-time part is registered with ETALIS (on line 4). From that time onwards the system is listening for events. The execution is blocked (on line 6) until events are detected. When new events are detected by ETALIS fulfilling the real-time part, the system starts collecting the historic parts of the query (starting on line 7) from the distributed backends. Querying historic data from backends (in the loop on line 8 ff.) is conducted in parallel. After that the results are sorted (on line 10) to optimise the following join. The nested-loop join (on line 11 ff.) finds a valid result satisfying all parts of the query or returns empty. If the join is non-empty (on line 13) then the combined results satisfy the overall query. The results are then used to derive the desired event (on line 14) according to the CONSTRUCT template in the query. Finally, the derived event is published. It can be received by subscribers and can match further queries. The algorithm is repeated (from line 5) and waits (i.e. is blocked) until new events arrive (on line 6). The loop, however, terminates if the query is unregistered by the user.

Algorithm 1 Query Execution for Hybrid Queries

```
query ← new query
rtQuery ← getRealTimePart(query)
histQueries[ ] ← getHistoricParts(query)
registerRealtimeQuery(rtQuery)                          ▷ Start detecting events

while isRegisteredRealtimeQuery(rtQuery) do
    rr ← new real-time result                           ▷ Event(s) detected
    hr[ ] ← empty array for historic results
    for all histQuery in histQueries[ ] do
        hr[ ] ←← append issueHistoricQuery(histQuery)
    hr[ ] ← orderBySize(hr[ ], ascending)
    for all hr in hr[ ] do
        rr ← rr ⋈ hr
    if rr ≠ ∅ then
        result ← createDerivedEvent(query, rr)
        publishEvent(result)                            ▷ Fire new event and repeat
```

This concludes the description of executing hybrid queries in our distributed system DCEP. The following section addresses the non-functional concern of permissions, e.g. who can subscribe to events and register queries for events.

7.3. Access Control

Our system has the requirement for multitenancy (cf. Requirement R17: *Multitenancy*). As such there is a need for privacy. Foremost, there is a need for annotating privacy on data (i.e. streams) such that users can define access to their real-time and historic information transmitted and stored in our system.

A further requirement for our system is to support open and extensible standards (Requirement R13: *Open Standards*). User management and access control are based on RDF. Therefore, the model of administrative information integrates seamlessly and in a standards-based way with the model for streams and events.

Data in our system is organised in streams (cf. topic-based publish/subscribe in Section 3.5). Attributing access control on a per-stream granularity was chosen. Finer granularity such as per-event attribution was discarded. The expected performance impact at runtime was thought to be unnecessarily high when having to check each event for each of its recipients before delivery. None of the scenarios required this granularity. Coarser granularity such as granting access to all streams at once, however, was contradicting Requirement R17: *Multitenancy* forfeiting the ability to separate users.

After analysing existing RDF models for access control (cf. Section 4.5) we concluded that *W3C WebAccessControl* was the most viable candidate of the three available candidates S4AC [Villata et al. 2011], SIOC Access [Berrueta 2010] and the W3C WebAccessControl [Berners-Lee 2009]. Reasons were its traction on the Web, its generality, and its ease of use[7] compared to the other candidates.

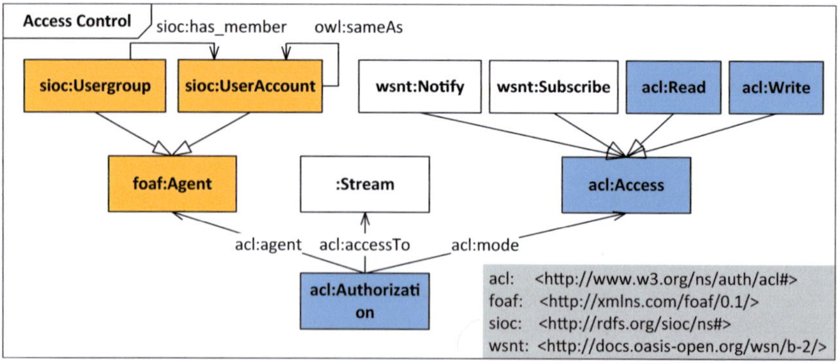

Figure 7.5.: Access Control Lists using the W3C WebAccessControl Vocabulary (Class Diagram)

[7] linking permissions with plain RDF resources instead of complex SPARQL queries

Figure 7.5 shows the concepts of WebAccessControl (WAC). The bottom of the figure shows that a single permission (`Authorization` in WAC terms) is a ternary relation. It consists of an agent (who can access), an information resource (what) and a mode (how), cf. middle row of the figure. An example ternary relation is: `Roland` can access the `TwitterFeed` with permissions `Subscribe` and `Read`. The top left of the figure shows an agent can be either a group or an individual user's account: User accounts can be members in groups. If accounts are defined in several locations, they can be declared to be the same, thus granting permissions to them all at once.

In Figure 7.5 the concepts from the WAC vocabulary are highlighted in blue colour. WAC has predefined access rights `Read` and `Write` for static data, cf. top right of the figure. For the use with real-time data we extended WAC with the rights `Notify` and `Subscribe`. The classes on white background in the figure are defined as part of this work. Finally, the classes in yellow are from the SIOC vocabulary.

```
@prefix acl:      <http://www.w3.org/ns/auth/acl#> .
@prefix foaf:     <http://xmlns.com/foaf/0.1/> .
@prefix group:    <http://groups.event-processing.org/id/> .
@prefix permission:  <http://permissions.event-processing.org/id/> .
@prefix person:   <http://www.roland-stuehmer.de/profile#> .
@prefix s:        <http://streams.event-processing.org/ids/> .
@prefix sioc:     <http://rdfs.org/sioc/ns#> .
@prefix wsnt:     <http://docs.oasis-open.org/wsn/b-2/> .

permission:p0001
      acl:accessTo s:TwitterFeed ;
      acl:agent person:rs ;
      acl:mode wsnt:Subscribe , acl:Read .

permission:p0002
      acl:accessTo s:FacebookStatusFeed ;
      acl:agent group:administrators ;
      acl:mode acl:Write .

person:rs
      sioc:member_of group:administrators ;
      owl:sameAs <http://data.semanticweb.org/person/roland-stuehmer> .
```

Listing 7.2: Permissions Example (Turtle Syntax)

Listing 7.2 shows two example authorizations p0001 and p0002 in the namespace permission starting on line 10 and 15. A user person:rs who is member of the group group:administrators is shown starting on line 20. Both permissions exhibit the ternary relation between who, what and how access is granted. The first permission states that Roland (rs) can access the TwitterFeed with permissions Subscribe and Read. The second permission states that group:administrators can access the FacebookStatusFeed with permission Write.

When defining permissions, the streams are modelled as information resources (e.g. http://.../TwitterFeed on line 11 without the trailing #stream). Elsewhere, streams are modelled with their non-information resource (e.g. http://.../TwitterFeed#stream). Making this distinction[8] we can attribute different metadata to the information for the stream (e.g. annotate permissions) and to the real-world stream (e.g. annotate its real-world event source or author).

RDF permissions like in Listing 7.2 are used in the access control module[9] of our system. The module checks whether to allow or deny access for the three parameters agent, resource and permission (who, what and how). To that end the module uses OWL reasoning and SPARQL Ask queries to arrive at its conclusion true (allow) or false (deny). By default we deny access if no known permissions are found.

OWL reasoning is employed as a preprocessing step before querying. We use OWL to infer relationships making use of transitive, inverse and symmetric properties of existing relationships between agents, resources and permissions. Doing so we can successfully grant access to (i) users who are in a group of a group which has access (**transitive** property sioc:member_of), (ii) users who have a group which lists them as member unilaterally (**inverse** properties sioc:member_of ↔ sioc:has_member) or (iii) users who have an equivalent user ID which has access (**symmetric** property owl:sameAs). For the relationships see Figure 7.5.

[8]See also our similar discussion for event URIs and the so-called *httpRange-14* issue in Section 5.3

[9]PLAY Commons library including play-commons-accesscontrol: https://github.com/play-project/play-commons/

A SPARQL `Ask` query is a Boolean type of query returning `true` if there are matching data in the dataset and `false` otherwise. We pose three disjunctive queries to arrive at the final conclusion (cf. line 5 of Algorithm 2) according to the WAC standard. First, we check if the supplied agent has **direct access** to a stream resource (line 6). Secondly, we check if the supplied agent has access via a **group membership** (line 8) and finally, we check whether the supplied agent has access via one of its RDF **classes** (line 10), which might be allowed to access. If none of the queries finds any matching permissions (all queries return false) we deny access, otherwise we allow access.

Algorithm 2 Evaluating Access Control

```
1: a ← agentUri                                        ▷ (who)
2: r ← resourceUri                                     ▷ (what)
3: p ← permissionUri                                   ▷ (how)
4: function CHECK(a, r, p)
5:     return CHECKDIRECTPERMISSION(a, r, p) ||
           CHECKVIAGROUPMEMBERSHIP(a, r, p) ||
           CHECKVIAAGENTCLASS(a, r, p)
6: function CHECKDIRECTPERMISSION(a, r, p)
7:     return SPARQL(
           ASK WHERE {
               [ acl:agent a ; acl:accessTo r ; acl:mode p ] })
8: function CHECKVIAGROUPMEMBERSHIP(a, r, p)
9:     return SPARQL(
           ASK WHERE {
               a sioc:member_of ?group .
               [ acl:agent ?group ; acl:accessTo r ; acl:mode p ] })
10: function CHECKVIAAGENTCLASS(a, r, p)
11:     return SPARQL(
           ASK WHERE {
               a rdf:type ?class .
               [ acl:agentClass ?class ; acl:accessTo r ; acl:mode p ] })
```

7.4. RESTful Services

The external interfaces of DCEP (cf. Section 7.2) are exposed as RESTful services. This is implemented in addition to the protocols WS-Notification and ProActive mentioned above. While the SOAP standard WS-Notification serves as a standardised protocol for publish/subscribe, the RESTful services described hereafter satisfy our requirements for exposing dereferenceable URIs (i.e. direct links) for things such as event patterns. Moreover, conventions in best practises of RESTful service design ease the rapid creation of client software such as the user interface described below to view, create, update and delete event patterns.

As mentioned in Section 3.3, REST relies on the limited set of "verbs" from HTTP 1.1 to describe actions which can be performed on URLs. Examples are get, put, delete and post. To manage event patterns in our system the `DcepManagementApi` exposes RESTful service URLs. The URLs and their supported verbs are listed in Table 7.1.

Table 7.1.: RESTful Services

URL	Verb	Description
/patterns	GET	fetch all entities
/patterns	POST	create entity
/patterns/id	GET	fetch entity
/patterns/id	PUT	modify entity
/patterns/id	DELETE	delete entity

The table shows how the service is designed to expose two kinds of URLs. The `/patterns` URL is a so-called collection URL. Interactions with it concern the entire collection of entities managed by the service. Individual entities in the collection are addressed by their so-called entity URLs. They are subordinate URLs according to their path template: `/patterns/id`.

All URLs represent resources uniquely. However, each unique resource such as an event pattern at `/patterns/1234` can be retrieved from the same endpoint in different syntactical variations. This is achieved through HTTP content negotiation[10]. A Web client can tell the Web server in the `Accept:` header which content type he/she prefers. Using this mechanism our system serves entities in several available content types. Supported types are JavaScript Object Notation (JSON), XML and plain text. Coining unique URIs supporting content negotiation for variants is addressing Requirement R8: *Linked Data Principles for Publishing*.

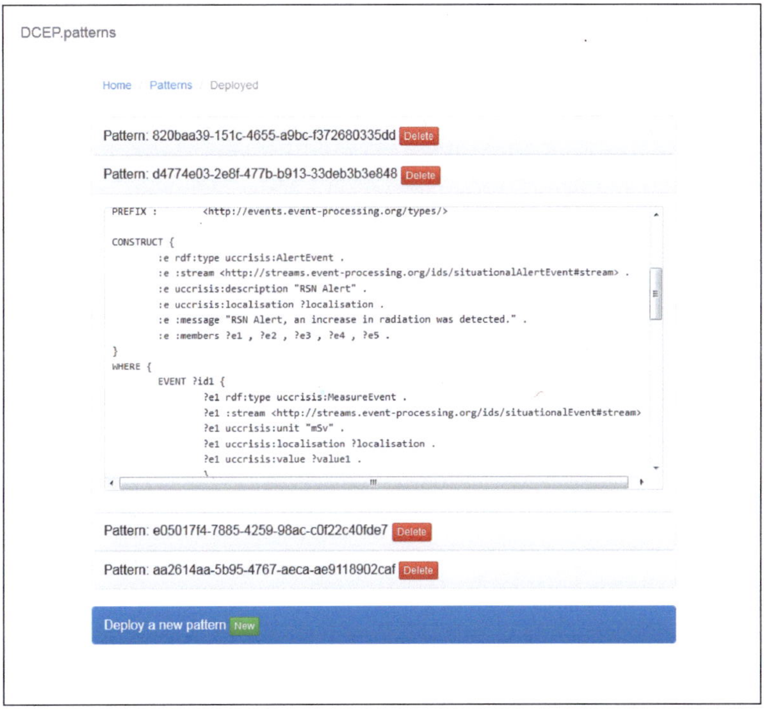

Figure 7.6.: RESTful Client using standardised JavaScript tooling

We created a graphical user interface to manage event patterns. It enables humans to interact with the RESTful `DcepManagementApi`. The entities

[10] HTTP 1.1 Content Negotiation: [Fielding et al. 1999, Section 12]

under management by our API are laid out according to clear conventions of RESTful service design as shown above. Therefore, generic management tools can be used. We employed Backbone.js[11] to create, update and delete entities in our service. Based on the exposed URL structure and JSON models, Backbone.js can be used to easily create user interfaces interacting with the collection and with individual entities.

Figure 7.6 shows the user interface based on Backbone.js. The view shows a list of entities, i.e. event patterns, currently in our system. The list was automatically generated by Backbone.js querying the collection URL of our REST API. Individual entities in the collection can be expanded to show the content of each entity in BDPL. The user interface can interact with the individual entity URLs via the "Delete" buttons in red. Furthermore, the interface can interact with the collection URL using the "New" button in green to create new entities in the collection of event patterns.

In conclusion, to satisfy Requirement R8: *Linked Data Principles for Publishing* we coined RESTful URLs for our management APIs to get unique, direct links to entities such as event patterns. Moreover, using REST conventions such as the predefined verbs, URL collection design and HTTP content negotiation we were able to create a standards-based user interface to interact with the API in a graphical way.

7.5. Linked Data Streaming

The Linked Data principles were introduced in Section 3.1 as four guidelines to model and publish data on the Web. In this thesis the principles are used to identify *context* for events as well as to provide a *publishing* paradigm. *Context* is described above in Section 5.3 modelling events and in Section 7.4 exposing related URIs, e.g. for event patterns in our platform. *Publishing* events according to Linked Data guidelines is discussed hereafter.

[11] Backbone.js: http://backbonejs.org/

Linked Data is described and implemented for static data in RDF but not for streaming data. Streaming data could also profit from the principles and the principles apply just as well.

Therefore, in this section we describe the design and implementation of our Linked Data streaming adapter. It is comprised of a Web server component which supports the streaming of RDF events in real-time. For this adapter, we designed an RDF streaming API to adapt the four Linked Data principles to real-time applications. Since our event format is built in RDF, the data modelling language fits seamlessly with the data dissemination. In analogy to the principles for static data [Berners-Lee 2006], the adapter follows these rules:

1. Use URIs to identify **streams**.
2. Use HTTP URIs so that these **streams** can be referred to and looked up by people and user agents.
3. When its URI is dereferenced, provide **real-time events from the stream** using standard formats such as RDF.
4. Include links to other, related URIs in the exposed **stream** to improve discovery of other related information on the Web.

Streams are potentially unbounded sequences of events. Thus, when accessing a stream URL the stream cannot be downloaded in one piece. To support the transmission of unbounded streams we use *persistent connections* from HTTP 1.1 [Fielding et al. 1999, Section 8.1]. The connections are kept alive and transmitting new events until the connections are closed explicitly.

Moreover, events occur spontaneously, thus, streams can exist which do not contain events at a constant rate. Therefore, we support the transmission of events at the discretion of the sender, i.e. whenever the event occurs. To that end we combine the persistent connections with *chunked transfer encoding* from HTTP 1.1 [Fielding et al. 1999, Section 3.6.1].

Chunked transfer encoding enables a Web server to start the transmission of content in chunks without knowing the final number and combined size of chunks. This knowledge is otherwise required for HTTP responses.

Instead, the server can transmit the data as a series of chunks, specifying only the size of each chunk as it is sent.

Another feature of streams is punctuation. "A punctuation is a pattern p inserted into the data stream with the meaning that no data item i matching p will occur further on in the stream" [Maier et al. 2005]. Punctuation provides guarantees to downstream components to make strong assumptions about what data has been received.

For event processing systems, events are the *fundamental* unit of information [Gupta and Jain 2011]. This means each event is processed atomically, i.e. completely or not at all. For RDF stream processing systems this can cause problems if events are modelled as graphs consisting of multiple quadruples: A receiver of an event must know with certainty that all quadruples pertaining to the event are transmitted in order to start processing the event.

In our system events are modelled as RDF graphs. Subsequently, graphs consist of RDF quadruples. Hence, for streams of RDF graphs punctuation can be re-interpreted as follows: A punctuation is a pattern p inserted into the quadruple stream with the meaning that no quadruples i from graph p will occur further on in the stream. This guarantee can be used by a downstream component to know that an event has been received in its entirety. The event can then be processed further in an atomic fashion.

Punctuation can be implemented using special ("magic") quadruples interweaved in the stream. However, since our system relies on the protocol stack of the Web, punctuation can be provided out-of-band, i.e. implemented on a lower layer of the stack. Thus, the RDF layer on top of our stack is not polluted with "magic" tokens. Rather, the underlying HTTP layer can support punctuation by means of *chunked transfer encoding* discussed previously. Each chunk is used to transfer exactly all quadruples of an event. The receipt of the chunk then indicates that an event is fully transferred or in other words guaranteeing that no quadruples from the event will arrive later.

Using the mechanism of chunked transfer encoding we created a server component (Linked Data streaming adapter) which keeps a connection alive when requested by a client. Whenever an event occurs in the server, a new chunk (with a known chunk size) is sent to the client and the connection is kept open. The combined chunk size of the unbounded stream needs not to be known, however, thus facilitating unbounded streaming of data using standard HTTP.

Using HTTP, our server can expose stream URIs and answer requests by sending events in real-time when they occur. Accessing a stream URI is not like a regular HTTP download of static, finite data but like a subscription to the stream. The subscription is started by accessing the URI for the desired stream. Then events are received by the client. The subscription can be ended by the client or the server terminating the persistent connection.

The advantage of the approach is that it is implemented using plain HTTP. No further client-side logic is required as in JavaScript-based approaches such as AJAX [Garrett 2005] and Comet [Russell 2006]. Thus, events are published in accordance with Linked Data principles addressing the rules mentioned above and fulfilling Requirement R8: *Linked Data Principles for Publishing*.

The adapter is integrated with our platform by connecting to the service bus (cf. Section 7.1). The address of the adapter is http://streams.event-processing.org to be able to resolve stream URIs used throughout this work. A stream URI like http://streams.event-processing.org/ids/TwitterFeed can now be directly dereferenced and the adapter is invoked.

When the adapter is invoked it replies with chunks of HTTP data, each chunk holding one event. The formatting of events can be controlled using HTTP content negotiation [Fielding et al. 1999, Section 12] as described above in Section 7.4. Content negotiation enables a client to specify which syntax of RDF is preferred using the `Accept:` header.

In conclusion, Linked Data is used in our work (i) as static context for events and (ii) as a means for publishing events dynamically in real-time:

- Context for events:
  - Additional information, e.g. everything in the Wikipedia such as people and place names
  - Structure for events, e.g. for geo data, coordinates

- Publishing of events:
  - HTTP URIs for historic events by ID
  - HTTP URIs for event streams by stream ID

The Linked Data streaming adapter is an output adapter, meaning it can be used by clients to obtain events from our platform. Events can be selected by stream. If a client knows a stream ID (e.g. from a historic event or from the WebApp catalogue of streams, cf. Section 7.7), the client can get a real-time feed of all current events in this stream using no other technology than plain HTTP and RDF.

The purpose of the Linked Data streaming adapter is to advance the principles of Linked Data towards real-time Linked Data.

7.6. Event Adapters

Not all events in our system were provided by the scenarios described in Section 2.7. To enable more diverse use cases and to alleviate a cold start of our system we add further real-time data sources. To that end we implemented several input adapters for well-known streaming data sources on the Web to be used by the scenarios.

Adding these existing sources of push-data addresses our Requirement R6: *Push-data on the Web.* We provide adapters for events from the Social Web as well as the Internet of Things (IoT) to demonstrate the diversity in existing data and the applicability of RDF to both fields.

Social Web sites such as Facebook and Twitter host a large amount of user-contributed material for a wide variety of events happening in the real-world. Events from Xively[12] further extend this range of events by adding real-time data from devices around the world which people are sharing.

Namely, these data sources include: (i) A Facebook app which a user can allow to notify all Facebook Wall updates as RDF events. (2) A Xively

[12]Xively, a Web portal to connect sensor data: http://xively.com/ previously known as Cosm and before that as Pachube

adapter which can subscribe to sensor readings and similar events from the IoT and can flexibly be transformed into RDF events. (3) A Twitter adapter which uses the Twitter API to receive tweets and convert them to RDF events.

The Facebook adapter. It consists of three modules. First, subscribing and retrieving the information from Facebook. Second, transforming this information to RDF events. Third, using WS-Notification publish/subscribe to deliver the events.

A Tomcat servlet is created for retrieving information and creating events. This application registers with Facebook to receive events in real-time. Whenever authenticated Facebook users post something on their Facebook Wall, a Facebook real-time notification is sent to our servlet using WebHooks. A WebHook is an HTTP callback: an HTTP POST request that occurs when something happens. The servlet then fetches the necessary data which is not part of the Facebook notification such as the user's location and the full message content. After that, the data is transformed into RDF events. Those events are sent to the service bus of our system for use in the platform.

Listing 5.1 on page 50 shows an example event from the Facebook adapter. The listing demonstrates the use of all attributes currently in the schema. Some attributes are in the default namespace of our system (e.g. `:status`), some are in the namespace `user:` [Weaver and Tarjan 2012] defined by the Facebook Graph API (e.g. `user:id`).

The Xively adapter. It has the purpose of subscribing to sensor readings and similar events from the IoT. Using the adapter, such events can be transformed into RDF events.

To connect Xively to the our system we implement another Java servlet. It is exposed to the Web in order for Xively to invoke it whenever there is new data using WebHooks. When the servlet is invoked, it parses the data received from Xively, converts it to RDF and creates an event instance using an event class from our SDK (cf. Section 5.4) specific to

Xively events. The data from Xively arrives as non-semantic JSON data. We lift the data to meaningful RDF from the structured JSON data in two consecutive steps according to [Norton and Krummenacher 2010]. The lifting is implemented as a SPARQL CONTRUCT query. First, JSON is converted to "naive" RDF by replicating only the structure, not the semantics. Then, CONSTRUCT queries are used like an RDF to RDF transformation. Meaningful RDF properties from well-known schemas can thereby be introduced in the event to increase interoperability between event producers and consumers. These properties replace the merely structural ones. This is done in order to make the results more usable as semantic events.

The Twitter adapter. It uses the Twitter API[13] to receive tweets and convert them to RDF events. To connect to the Twitter API we have implemented another dedicated Java servlet. It makes heavy use of the Twitter4J[14] library, a Java library for the Twitter API. The Twitter API "allows high-throughput near real-time access to various subsets of public and protected Twitter data". Public tweets are available from all users, filtered in various ways: By user id, by keyword, by random sampling and/or by geographic location.

Listing 7.3 shows an example Twitter event displaying properties from our schema. As a best practice in ontology design we not only define our own schema but re-use existing schemas to increase interoperability with other software and increase semantic understanding of our data. This addresses our Requirement R5: *Ontology re-use*. Thus, our schema uses event properties from the namespace `sioc:` in the SIOC ontology[15] on line 21 to describe user generated content on the Web 2.0. Moreover, we reuse properties from the W3C Basic Geo Vocabulary[16] in the namespace `geo:` on lines 18 and 19 to describe the location in a standardised way.

[13]Twitter API: https://dev.twitter.com/

[14]Twitter4J, Java library for the Twitter API: http://twitter4j.org/

[15]SIOC Core Ontology Specification: http://sioc-project.org/ontology

[16]Basic Geo (WGS84 lat/long) Vocabulary: http://www.w3.org/2003/01/geo/

```
@prefix :        <http://events.event-processing.org/types/> .
@prefix e:       <http://events.event-processing.org/ids/> .
@prefix geo:     <http://www.w3.org/2003/01/geo/wgs84_pos#> .
@prefix sioc:    <http://rdfs.org/sioc/ns#> .
@prefix xsd:     <http://www.w3.org/2001/XMLSchema#> .

e:twitter39043305504377175 {
  <http://events.event-processing.org/ids/twitter39043305504377175#
      event>
    a :TwitterEvent ;
    :endTime "2011-06-02T15:06:45.000Z"^^xsd:dateTime ;
    :followersCount  "10"^^xsd:int ;
    :friendsCount "1"^^xsd:int ;
    :isRetweet "false"^^xsd:boolean ;
    :screenName "softamo" ;
    :stream <http://streams...org/ids/TwitterFeed#stream> ;
    :twitterName "Sergio del Amo" ;
    :location [
      geo:lat     "43.616231774652796"^^xsd:double;
      geo:long  "7.053824782139356"^^xsd:double
    ] ;
    sioc:content "Animate a participar en el programa @wayra de
        Telefonica y consigue apoyo integral para tu proyecto http://
        bit.ly/k84qgN #iniciador" .
}
```

Listing 7.3: Example of a Twitter Event (TriG Syntax)

7.7. Web Application

Events are often consumed by specialised, domain specific programmes. However, in some cases there is the need to view all raw events as-is, in an ad-hoc fashion. This is true, e.g. for developers debugging event streams or for end users discovering available event streams. In such cases events must be viewed but not fully interpreted by machines.

We developed a Web application, called the *WebApp*[17]. It enables users to browse streams, view RDF events in real-time and browse historic events.

The WebApp demonstrates our notion of an event marketplace. It is a system where producers of events make their events known and consumers

[17]WebApp Source Code: https://github.com/play-project/WebApp

look for available events (cf. Section 2.6). Events can be searched based on static information (i.e. stream metadata) and can be viewed based on their dynamic content (i.e. event payloads).

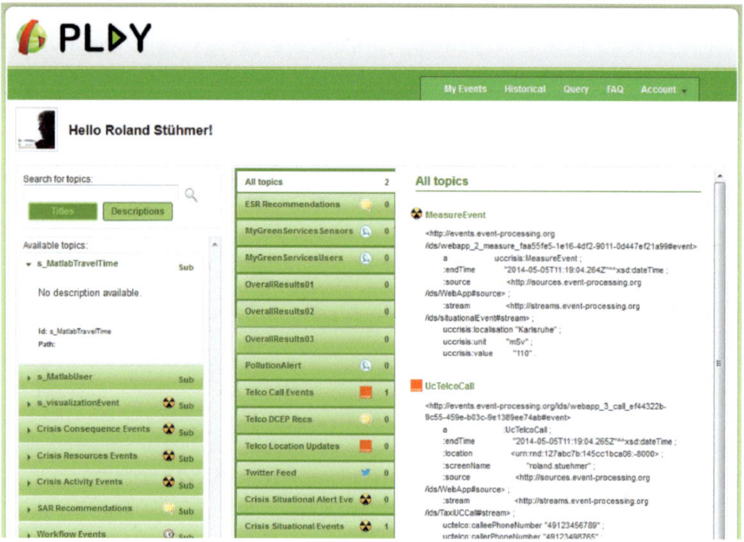

Figure 7.7.: Web Application: Event Marketplace View

Figure 7.7 shows a screenshot of the main page of our WebApp. Static stream data can be seen in the left column. Subscribed streams can be seen in the centre column. Dynamic event content can be seen in the right column.

The left column shows static stream metadata. The metadata is modelled by stream providers in RDF. The schema for streams contains a human-readable and internationalised title, long description, a stream icon and the unique stream URL. The schema was presented as part of our RDF model in Section 5.3. The textual metadata can be searched using the box at the top of the left column in the figure.

The centre column shows the subscribed streams. To view dynamic event data in the WebApp a stream must be subscribed. This happens when clicking on the "Sub" link of a stream in the left column, thus moving the stream into the centre column, subscribing to it.

The rightmost column shows the dynamic content of the subscribed streams. The displayed events are shown for all subscribed streams or for just one stream depending on what is selected in the centre column. Events are displayed in a mostly raw format. No domain-specific schemas are employed by the WebApp to render events; however, the generic schema from our model is used: the event type is rendered as headline, and the event icon URI is used to find and display icons in the right column.

To show events in real-time efficiently the WebApp is implemented using dynamic JavaScript technology. Thus, events can be notified by our Web server to the Web clients immediately when the events occur. The WebApp is connected to the service bus of our platform (cf. Section 7.1) to receive events. To minimise network bandwidth the WebApp subscribes to each stream only once even if several clients subscribe to the same stream. Events of each stream are then demultiplexed by the WebApp for each client. The WebApp only unsubscribes from a stream with the service bus when the last client has unsubscribed from the stream.

In conclusion, the search functionality in the WebApp enables users to search for interesting streams based on keywords in the textual metadata. Streams can be found and sampled in real-time using the WebApp.

7.8. Discussion

Table 7.2 summarises the coverage of requirements from Chapter 2 by the design decisions made above. The table distinguishes only three main design decisions for the sake of simplicity. The first is the subsumption of all decisions which influence the **DCEP Component** (third column from the right). The second design decision subsumes the decisions made for the **WebApp** component (second column from the right). The third design decision depicted in the table subsumes all design decisions taken for the event **Adapters and SDKs** (rightmost column).

Table 7.2.: Overview of Requirements for the Infrastructure

Requirement	Fulfilled by: DCEP Component	Fulfilled by: WebApp	Fulfilled by: Adapters, SDK
R1: *Events are first-class objects*	✓		✓
R6: *Push-data on the Web*			✓
R8: *Linked Data Principles for Publishing*			✓
R10: *Hybrid Querying*	✓		
R12: *Infrastructure*	✓	✓	✓
R13: *Open Standards*	✓		
R14: *Event-driven*	✓		
R15: *Adaptivity*	✓		
R16: *Event Metadata*		✓	
R17: *Multitenancy*	✓		
R20: *Support for Programmers*		✓	✓

Table 7.2 can be understood line by line: The requirement *Events are first-class objects* is fulfilled by our design of the DCEP component as well as the adapters which produce atomic, first-class event objects for every update they detect. *Push-data on the Web* can be consumed in our infrastructure thanks to the respective event adapters. *Linked Data Principles for Publishing* are employed by the Linked Data streaming adapter described above. *Hybrid Querying* is made possible by the DCEP component whereas *Infrastructure* is generally provided by all three components. *Open Standards* are introduced mainly by the DCEP component but also used elsewhere in the WebApp and Adapters to a lesser degree. The requirement of being *Event-driven* is again mainly fulfilled by the design of DCEP. The same holds true for *Adaptivity* which enables users to register and

unregister event queries at any time and introduce new schemas in event bodies at any time. *Event Metadata* for event streams is made searchable by the WebApp component, thus fulfilling this requirement. *Multitenancy* is supported by DCEP with the ability of enforcing access control through governance. *Support for Programmers*, finally, is provided by the SDK to help programming RDF in Java.

8 Evaluation

In this chapter we evaluate the artefacts produced as part of this work. Firstly, the fulfilment of all requirements is verified. Secondly, a popular event processing scenario is implemented using our approach to validate the necessary expressiveness. Then, the overall cost of the Web-based approach is determined compared to a non-Web-based solution. After that, qualitative comparisons are made with the State of the Art followed by a quantitative performance analysis of the overall infrastructure through stress tests.

8.1. Fulfilment of Requirements

As the first part of our evaluation we recapitulate all requirements from Chapter 2 and track if and how they are fulfilled. Table 8.1 summarises the coverage of all requirements by the combined design decisions made for our main contributions in Chapters 5 to 7. The fulfilment of requirements was discussed above for each contribution separately. This table is the combined conclusion.

Table 8.1.: Overview of all Requirements for this Work

Requirement	Fulfilled by
R1: *Events are first-class objects*	The design of class `Event` in our model enables standalone instances for events (Section 5.3)
R2: *Time properties*	The definition of time properties in our model (Section 5.3)
R3: *Type hierarchy*	Use of RDFS to enable hierarchies and our own classes implementing a hierarchy (Section 5.3)
R4: *Inter-event relationships*	Link properties like `:member` in our model (Section 5.3) to reference related events on an instance level
R5: *Ontology re-use*	Schemas like DOLCE, W3C Geo, SSN, WebAccessControl re-used by our model and infrastructure (Section 5.5.1)
R6: *Push-data on the Web*	Adapters for existing real-time data, e.g. for Xively (Section 7.6)
R7: *Linked Data Principles for Modelling*	Link properties like `:stream` in our model to reference and locate further data (Section 5.3)
R8: *Linked Data Principles for Publishing*	Linked Data streaming adapter to serve real-time data when dereferencing a stream URI (Section 7.5)
R9: *Support for the data model*	Use of SPARQL as a starting point for our language (Chapter 6)

Continued on next page

Requirement	Fulfilled by
	Continued from last page
R10: *Hybrid Querying*	Our extensions to SPARQL (Section 6.3) and our federated execution (Section 7.2.3)
R11: *Temporal Operators*	Our extensions to SPARQL (Section 6.3)
R12: *Infrastructure*	All components: DCEP (Section 7.2), WebApp (Section 7.7), Adapters (Section 7.6)
R13: *Open Standards*	Use of RDF and RDFS (Section 3.1), extension of SPARQL (Section 6.3), REST services (Section 7.4), WS-Notification (Section 7.1.2)
R14: *Event-driven*	Our extensions to SPARQL (Section 6.3) and our implementation of the DCEP event processing engine (Section 7.2)
R15: *Adaptivity*	Adding and removing patterns at run time (Section 7.2), flexibility of RDFS at design time (Section 3.1)
R16: *Event Metadata*	Use of RDF to define metadata (Section 5.3) and WebApp to search metadata (Section 7.7)
R17: *Multitenancy*	Definition and enforcement of access control (Section 7.3)
R18: *Query Expressivity*	Use of SPARQL and our extensions (Section 2.7)
R19: *Mobility*	Property `:location` in our model (Section 5.3)
R20: *Support for Programmers*	SDK (Section 5.4), predefined and abstract event adapter implementations (Section 7.6)

In conclusion, Table 8.1 shows that each requirement from Chapter 2 is fulfilled by at least one design decision made for this work.

8.2. Efficiency of the Approach

As the next step of the evaluation we examine the issue of the computational cost incurred by RDF event processing. To that end we compare our work with a non-RDF event processing system as the baseline.

As part of our system we developed a native RDF event processor. That means RDF events are understood as-is, without transformation. This has the benefit of preserving all semantics of RDF throughout our system. We want to evaluate the performance cost of that. Our event processor is implemented using the underlying event processor ETALIS. We re-use its temporal event operators but we add RDF capabilities[1].

To measure the runtime cost of our additions to the basic ETALIS system we ran similar experiments on both systems and compared the throughput of both cases. We created two similar event patterns, one in BDPL and one in ETALIS Language for Events (ELE), the native language of ETALIS. Each pattern matched and consumed every single event of a given type, i.e. the garbage collection was fully tested. The defined pattern in each language was designed for each simulated simple event (input) to create one complex event (output). We then compared the output rates for each approach. The simple events were created at the highest possible speed of each experiment so that the Java buffers were always full. One hundred thousand simple events of the same type were created during the course of each part of the experiment.

The experimental setup used a Core Duo 2.0 GHz with 3 GB RAM running Windows7 32bit, SWI Prolog 5.10.5, Java 1.6 and a Java heap size of 256 MB. The experiments ran locally on the machine, eliminating the influence of networking as part of the setup.

Figure 8.1 shows the results. On the x-axis are all simulated events from the first one on the left of the figure to the 100,000th on the right. The y-axis shows the frequency of complex events created per second. As mentioned before, for each simple event exactly one complex event is

[1] Please note that there was one previous, independent approach to adding RDF to ETALIS called EP-SPARQL. We do not build on top of EP-SPARQL because of its simpler event model. Cf. the discussion in Section 4.6.

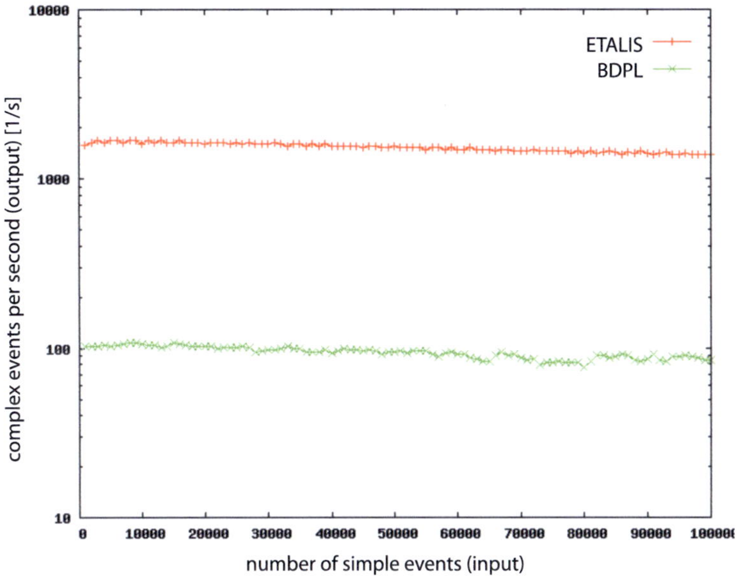

Figure 8.1.: Efficiency of the Approach (Throughput of BDPL compared with non-RDF ETALIS)

produced. This incurs a delay which is measured. The two curves describe the experiments, BDPL with RDF support and plain ETALIS rules without RDF support. Both curves are nearly constant showing that both engines do proper garbage collection so that consumed events do not slow down the engines over time during the course of the experiment. Throughout the experiment the performance of BDPL is about ten times lower than that of the plain event processing engine, i.e. one can conclude that the cost of RDF event processing for the current state of the implementation is about one order of magnitude higher than for event processing without RDF.

This cost is incurred for the expressiveness of RDF, its self-descriptiveness, the extensibility and distributed ownership of schemas and the possibility of exploiting Web data in events. Technically, RDF events are much more verbose than events for plain ETALIS. An ETALIS event looks like the following example, `event(myEvent('Hello World', 5.1, 5), datime(Y, M,D,H,Min,S))` where `myEvent` is the event type followed by zero or more unnamed properties of simple Prolog data types (in this case string, decimal and integer) and followed by one or two timestamps (in this case one timestamp for point-based events).

RDF events on the other hand (cf. example in Listing 5.1 on page 50) have several features which increase the verbosity (i.e. the size and parsing effort) of payloads: (i) named properties which allow the departure from fixed, comma-separated schemas as in Prolog, (ii) the use of HTTP URIs for identifiers which facilitate globally unique identification of schema documents and (iii) the use of explicit typing of properties from the XML Schema type system which is more expressive than the simple types of Prolog and other programming languages. These are some of the building blocks for creating Web-oriented interoperability (cf. Requirement R5: *Ontology re-use*).

In conclusion, the use of native RDF in event processing incurs a runtime cost of about one order of magnitude in terms of decreased throughput. This has to be taken into account when weighting the advantages of such a system and of RDF. During the realisation of our scenarios (cf. Section 2.7) we found that 100 events per second are sufficient for all their use cases.

8.3. Comparison with Related Work

The benchmark SRBench [Zhang et al. 2012] allows qualitative comparisons between RDF streaming engines. The benchmark compares previous RDF streaming solutions $\text{SPARQL}_{\text{Stream}}$, CQELS and C-SPARQL (cf. Chapter 4 for a discussion of the state of the art). Quantitative comparisons such as latency and throughput are not conducted by SRBench. To fulfil SRBench there are 17 queries to be modelled, Q1 to Q17. Each is characterised by one or more language features needed to support the expressivity of the SRBench scenario.

Table 8.2.: Query Expressivity of BDPL compared to the State of the Art

	Q1	Q2	Q3	Q4	Q5	Q6	Q7	Q8	Q9	Q10	Q11	Q12	Q13	Q14	Q15	Q16	Q17
$\text{SPARQL}_{\text{Stream}}$	✓	PP	A	G	G	✓	✓	G	G, IF	SD	SD	PP, SD	PP, SD	PP, SD	PP, SD	PP, SD	PP, SD
CQELS	✓	PP	A	✓	✓	✓	D/ N	✓	IF	✓	✓	PP	PP	PP	PP	PP	PP
C-SPARQL	✓	PP	A	✓	✓	✓	D	✓	IF	✓	✓	PP	PP	PP	PP	PP	PP
BDPL	✓	✓ (1, 2)	A	SM (3)	✓	✓ (4)	✓	SM	SM	✓	✓ (5)	PP, SM	✓ (6, 7)	✓	✓	✓	✓

Table 8.2 shows the resulting feature matrix extended with our approach, BDPL. Check marks denote fully supported queries. Abbreviations denote a missing feature why a particular query is not fully supported by one of the approaches: A: Ask query form, D: Dstream, G: groupBy and aggregations, IF: if expression, N: negation, PP: property path, SD: static dataset, all abbreviations defined in [Zhang et al. 2012]. We added SM: no solutions modifiers implemented yet (e.g. MIN(?values) in CONSTRUCT clause).

Implementation of a streaming query like in this benchmark is often not straightforward and the natural language definitions of the queries leave room for interpretation. Where appropriate we leave some technical implementation notes: (1) property paths in the query Q2 can be replaced by RDFS reasoning in our implementation, (2) optional parts currently return a placeholder value instead of UNDEF, (3) results are reported not every 10 minutes but updated on each event (sliding window is used), (4) UNION can be replaced by BDPL AND-operator here, (5) subselect can be replaced by BDPL SEQ-operator here, (6) disjunctive property path replaced by BDPL OR-operator here, (7) property paths in historical part are allowed in BDPL, as we have higher expressivity here thanks to federation of historical queries which have the full expressivity of SPARQL 1.1 including property paths.

Discussing the benchmark, it becomes apparent that some important features of our work are not evaluated such as the event model allowing expressive events to be notified or federated queries allowing large quantities of historical data to be incorporated in results. Also, ASK queries (as marked by "A" in Table 8.2) are part of the benchmark but are not useful in event processing as they return Boolean query results, not structured derived events. We discussed this in Section 6.3.

In conclusion, our implementation ranks above average when counting the check marks in Table 8.2, a benchmark comparing the language expressivity of the state of the art in RDF event processing.

8.4. Overall System Test

The overall system is evaluated in terms of scenario-based tests. The questions to be answered are:

- What is the latency for each individual component as the event throughput increases?
- What is the overall (end-to-end) latency as the event throughput increases?

The scenarios use real-world data collected from Twitter and match several synthetic patterns on them. Two experiments were conducted using the same event patterns but varying datasets and speeds. We first describe the origin and structure of the datasets below followed by the structure and purpose of each event pattern. After that we introduce the two experimental setups and their results.

The components under test are "event processing" and "storage" from Figure 7.1 on page 74. The component "service bus" is used in our experimental setup to send and receive events but the throughput is only measured for the core components event processing and storage. Our component DCEP is used for event processing. The third-party component EventCloud[2] [Pellegrino et al. 2013] is used for storage. EventCloud

[2]EventCloud: http://eventcloud.inria.fr/

is a distributed publish/subscribe system to store and forward RDF data in real-time like an active database. Both components are involved in answering hybrid queries of real-time and historic data.

The tests were run on a machine with 8 cores Intel Xeon CPU E7–4860 at 2.27 GHz, 24 GB of main memory, 500 GB of disk space running Fedora Linux release 17 (Beefy Miracle).

8.4.1. Test Dataset

The experiments were conducted with recorded events to be able to reproduce[3] the results. Events have been recorded from Twitter in June 2013 during seven consecutive days. Four different simple event streams have been collected with arbitrary but popular keywords in the message. The keywords were `google`, `apple`, `microsoft` and `yahoo`. Using our event adapter for Twitter (cf. Section 7.6) we lifted the tweets to RDF.

The event types in RDF are subclasses of `TwitterEvent`, namely G, A, M and Y respectively for the four kinds of tweets. The event instances contain properties such as the originating Twitter user, the tweet message and the number of friends the originating twitter user has.

We have collected 23.200 events in total, i.e. 5.800 of each type. Listing 8.1 shows an example event of type `google` (cf. line 9). Each event consisted of twelve RDF statements (triples) on average and amounted to 1428 bytes on average.

Variations in event size are due to the varying nature of the basic data from twitter, e.g. the message length which is depicted by the event property `sioc:content` on line 18 of Listing 8.1.

Variations in the number of triples per event result from our modelling of properties. For example like the data supplied by the Twitter API we model a separate property for each link detected in a tweet. This number can vary. The property `sioc:links_to` from the SIOC ontology is used

[3]Test dataset: https://github.com/play-project/play-test/tree/develop/play-test-overall-scenario-simulator. See also Appendix A.1 on open-source artefacts.

for this purpose. One such property is depicted on line 10 of the listing. Since the number of links in a tweet can vary, the number of triples varies depending on the number of links detected in an original tweet. Similar modelling is used for hashtags and users' names mentioned in a tweet resulting in further variability of the number of triples per event.

The dataset can be replayed at varying data rates to perform the stress tests of the platform.

```
1  @prefix :    <http://events.event-processing.org/types/> .
2  @prefix e:     <http://events.event-processing.org/ids/> .
3  @prefix sioc: <http://rdfs.org/sioc/ns#> .
4  @prefix xhtml2: <http://www.w3.org/2002/06/xhtml2/> .
5  @prefix xsd:  <http://www.w3.org/2001/XMLSchema#> .
6
7  e:twitter_2e7586a0-7f9a-4181-91ed-110e5a57aa79 {
8    <http://events...org/ids/twitter_2e7586a0-...-110e5a57aa79#event>
9      a :google ;
10     sioc:links_to <http://t.co/b> ;
11     :userMention "MaxenceDodi" , "Estirpe_" , "hematocritico" , "
           NoelBurgundy" ;
12     :endTime "2013-07-22T09:17:01.000Z"^^xsd:dateTime ;
13     :stream <http://streams...org/ids/TwitterFeed#stream> ;
14     :source <http://sources...org/ids/TwitterAdapter#source> ;
15     :friendsCount "322"^^xsd:int ;
16     :followersCount "6231"^^xsd:int ;
17     :isRetweet "true"^^xsd:boolean ;
18     sioc:content "RT @MaxenceDodi: Esta tarde a las 18h Google Hangout
           con el equipo de @estirpe_ acompanados de @hematocritico y
           @NoelBurgundy http://t.co/b" ;
19     :screenName "NoelBurgundy" ;
20     :twitterName "Noel Ceballos" ;
21     xhtml2:icon <http://www.google.de/favicon.ico> .
22 }
```

Listing 8.1: Scenario-based Test: Example Event (TriG Syntax)

8.4.2. Test Patterns

For the experiments three synthetic event patterns were created. The goal was to provide a realistic query load. The patterns are based on the event types G, A, M and Y mentioned above. The patterns are of increasing complexity to provide realistic runtime behaviour.

The first pattern matches G, A, M and Y in sequence (i.e. one event *strictly* following the other) within a time window of five seconds. This pattern was chosen with the goal of stress testing the temporal matching of the event processing engine. Cf. Listing 8.2.

```
#
# Basic pattern detecting 4 company-related events in sequence.
#

CONSTRUCT {
  :e rdf:type :UcTelcoEsrRecom .
  :e :stream <http://.../ids/OverallResults01#stream> .
  :e uctelco:ackRequired "false"^^xsd:boolean .
  :e uctelco:answerRequired "false"^^xsd:boolean .
  :e :message "Pattern 01: Four tweets were detected."^^xsd:string .
}
WHERE {
  WINDOW {
    EVENT ?id1 {
      ?e1 rdf:type :google .
      ?e1 :stream <http://.../ids/TwitterFeed#stream> .
      ?e1 :screenName ?screenName01 .
      }
    SEQ
    EVENT ?id2 {
      ?e2 rdf:type :apple .
      ?e2 :stream <http://.../ids/TwitterFeed#stream> .
      }
    SEQ
    EVENT ?id3 {
      ?e3 rdf:type :microsoft .
      ?e3 :stream <http://.../ids/TwitterFeed#stream> .
      }
    SEQ
    EVENT ?id4 {
      ?e4 rdf:type :yahoo .
      ?e4 :stream <http://.../ids/TwitterFeed#stream> .
      }
  } ("PT5S"^^xsd:duration, sliding)
}
```

Listing 8.2: Scenario-based Test: First Pattern (BDPL Syntax)

The second pattern is a specialisation of the first pattern to be more selective. It matches a subset of the matched events from the first pattern and is more complex to calculate. The pattern matches each event G, A, M and Y only if it is from a Twitter user with more than ten followers. This pattern was chosen to stress test the content-based filtering capability of the event processing engine.

The third pattern is another specialisation of the first pattern. It matches the real-time results with historic data. The pattern detects the subset of the same events where the originating Twitter user of one Tweet (in our case A) had been tweeting in the past. This pattern was chosen to stress test the cost of retrieving historic data from storage and joining it with the real-time data in memory.

The full text of all three patters can be found in Appendix B: Listings B.1 to B.3.

8.4.3. Experiments

Based on the events and patterns described above we conducted two experiments. The first experiment runs a small dataset with all components at differing speeds. The second experiment tests all components with a larger dataset and therefore high stress on historical queries testing at two different speeds. Each dataset is run at increasing speeds by consecutively shortening a delay when replaying the events. The delay is decreased down to 0 ms, the burst transmission. Each measurement is repeated three times to get a meaningful average reading for every single datapoint in the experiments.

- First Experiment
  - Numbers of tests: 10
  - Dataset: 400 events
  - **Delay between the transmissions** of events by the simulator: 200 ms, 100 ms, 50 ms, 25 ms, 12 ms, 6 ms, 3 ms, 1 ms, 0 ms
  - Repeat each experiment three times in order to calculate the mean processing time for DCEP and Storage
- Second Experiment
  - Numbers of tests: 2
  - **Dataset:** 23.200 events
  - Delay between the transmissions of events by the simulator: 6 ms, 0 ms

The previous list summarises the two experiments. Notable differences are in bold print.

8.4.4. Results

Figure 8.2 shows results from the **first experiment**. The components under test are event processing (DCEP) and storage (EventCloud). The x-axis shows the increasing transmission speed of the incoming events. The y-axis shows the latency for each outgoing event, i.e. for EventCloud the time difference for an event passing through the component and for DCEP the time difference between a complex event leaving the component and the last of its simple events having entered the component.

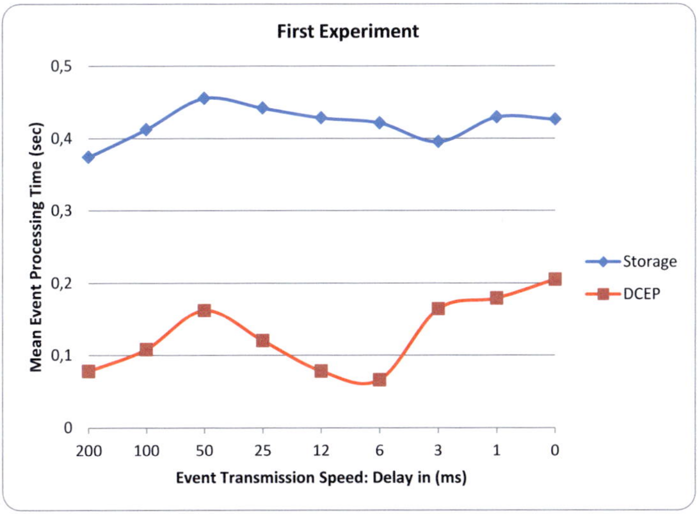

Figure 8.2.: Mean Event Processing Time vs. Event Transmission Speed in the First Experiment (Line Chart)

The transmission speeds are increased from low throughput, using a delay of 200 ms between sending events at the datasource up to about 256 times that speed, using no delay between sending events at the datasource.

At increasing transmission speeds storage shows an almost constant processing time. DCEP, however, shows an increasing processing time. We cannot explain the fluctuation between 50 ms delay and 6 ms delay even though we conducted the experiment repeatedly as explained above. The general increase in transmission speed, however, is explained as follows: The experiments define event patterns with time windows of five seconds (Section 8.4.2). At increasing event speeds these time windows match more and more events occurring within the length of a window. This has two implications for the performance of an event processing system:

(i) The memory consumption increases as more events are valid at any given time as part of the matching windows. Thus, these events cannot be removed from memory by garbage collection.

(ii) When deriving the resulting complex event from such a match, more data (i.e. all valid events in the window) must be taken into account. Thus, the result becomes larger and longer to compute.

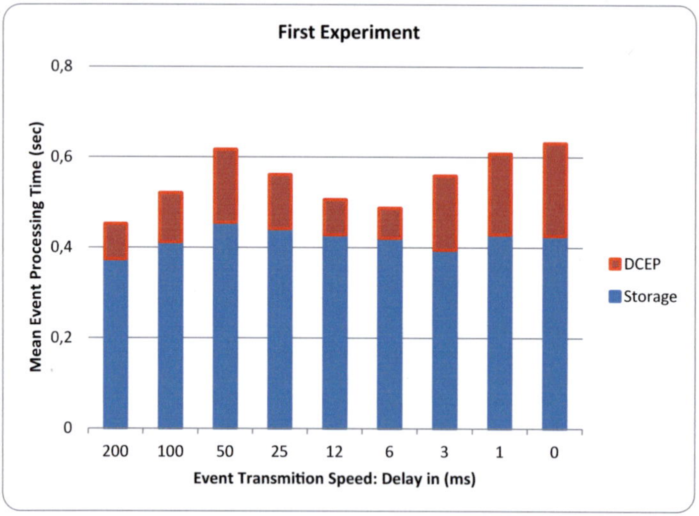

Figure 8.3.: Accumulated (stacked) Mean Event Processing Time vs. Event Transmission Speed in the First Experiment (Stacked Bar Chart)

Figure 8.3 shows that, overall, the combined system scales satisfactorily from the slow experiment (used as a reference speed) on the left of the figure all the way to the burst experiment on the right. On average the latency of both components combined is 0.549 sec for the first experiment, cf. Table 8.3.

Table 8.3.: Mean Event Processing Time in the First Experiment

	Avg. Latency		Std. Dev.
	[ms]	[%]	σ [ms]
Storage:	0.420	77 %	0.023
DCEP:	0.129	23 %	0.047
Total:	0.549	100 %	

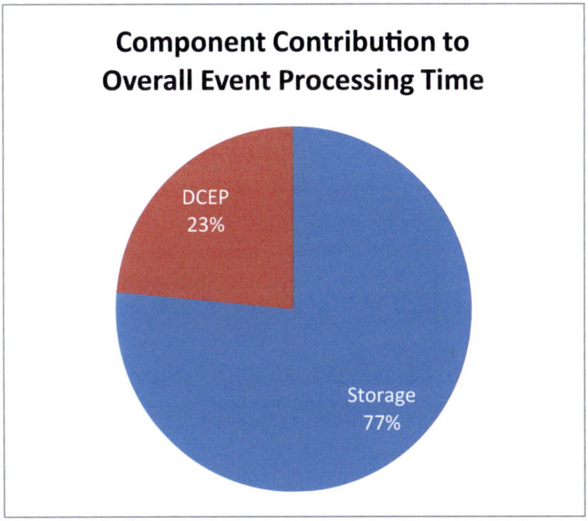

Figure 8.4.: Mean Component Contribution to Overall Event Processing Time in the First Experiment (Pie Chart)

After looking at the average of the combined system we look at the components individually. Table 8.3 shows the details of latency per component. For storage the average latency in the first experiment is 0.420 ms or 77 % of the total. For DCEP it is 0.129 ms or 23 %.

The pie chart of Figure 8.4 shows the percentages of the contribution of each component to the overall latency of the system. These percentages change in the second experiment when a larger dataset is used.

Figure 8.5 shows the event processing times for the **second experiment**. As stated above, two speeds were tested using the larger dataset. The dataset was increased from 400 events in the first experiment to 23.200 events in the second experiment. The figure shows that a lot more latency is incurred in DCEP than in storage now. Figure 8.6 confirms this, showing 89 % of the total latency contributed by DCEP as opposed to just 23 % with the smaller dataset in the first experiment, above. Storage shows almost the same mean event processing time, with a small increase in the end because of the growing history storing the large dataset.

The growing number of historic events is specific to the second experiment. The event pattern with a historic part is pattern number three (cf. Listing B.3 in Appendix B, indicated by the existence of a GRAPH clause on line 46). Thus, it is affected by historic events.

The GRAPH clause in pattern three requests all previous (historic) tweets of the same author who posted the `apple` tweet as part of the pattern. This means that while the history of events grows during the experiment the historic results for this query grow as well.

However, since the dispatch of historical queries and joining of their results with the real-time data is a task of DCEP (cf. Section 7.2.3), the long delays for hybrid queries are entirely attributed to DCEP.

The latency attributed to storage in Figures 8.5 and 8.6 is comprised only of the transmission of real-time events. Historic queries are not part of the latency we detected for storage. Historic queries only indirectly slowed down the storage component by a small latency increase in the end but the effect is invisible in the figure.

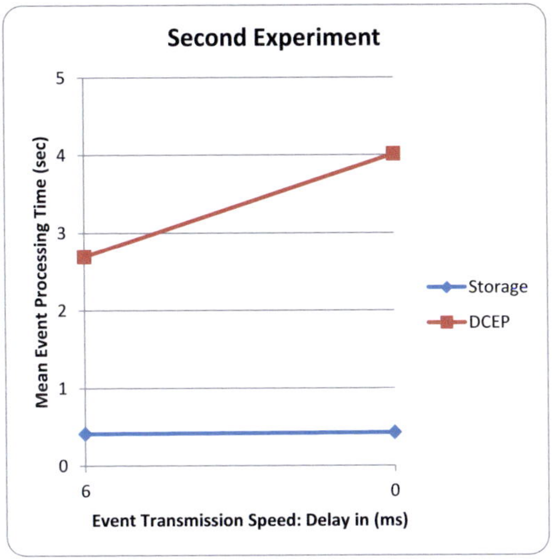

Figure 8.5.: Mean Event Processing Time vs. Event Transmission Speed in the Second Experiment (Line Chart)

On the other hand, the increase in latency for DCEP in the end (right side of Figure 8.5) is the known effect from the first experiment of higher event frequencies coupled with time windows: More events per second means that a five second time window matches more events at any given time. This results in higher memory consumption for DCEP and higher load because of larger result sets.

In conclusion, Figure 8.3 shows that, overall, the combined system scales satisfactorily. Nevertheless, the artificial event patterns from the experimental setup must be optimised to be appropriate for growing histories of events. This could be achieved by increasing the selectivity of the historic part much like the real-time part has a high selectivity by having a constrained time window.

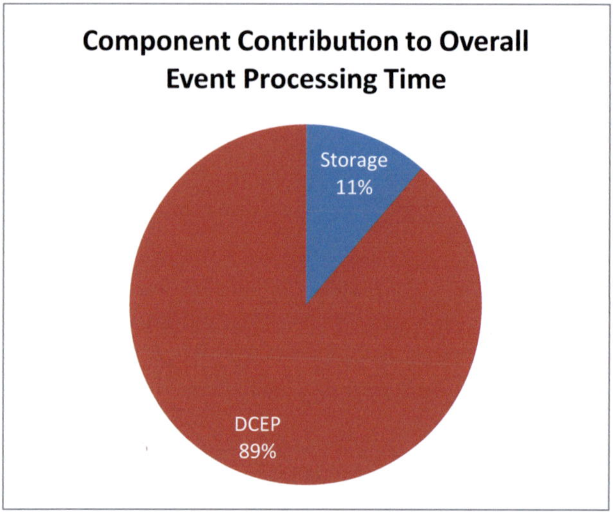

Figure 8.6.: Mean Component Contribution to Overall Event Processing Time in the Second Experiment (Pie Chart)

8.5. Fast Flower Delivery Scenario

The fast flower delivery scenario is an example event processing application from the book [Etzion and Niblett 2010]. The purpose of the scenario is to illustrate features commonly found in event processing applications.

The scenario may be used to validate the expressivity of existing event processing systems. This was done for several related systems before, e.g. in [Aničić 2012, Section 13.2.1] and [Weidlich et al. 2013]. We implemented parts of the scenario for our language BDPL.

The scenario is described in [Etzion and Niblett 2010, Appendix B] using five phases of a fictional flower delivery process, including the situations to be detected, the schema of events and the sequence of events.

A fictional consortium of flower shops outsources their flower deliveries to local, independent van drivers. Drivers are ranked according to their previous performance. In the first phase of the scenario ("bid phase") a shop emits an event indicating that a new delivery is to be made. According to background data about drivers' rankings a central system in the scenario sends events to only those drivers who match minimum requirements. In the second phase ("assignment phase") the drivers may respond with a bid on the delivery. They have two minutes to do so until the central system aggregates all occurring bids and creates a report with the five highest-ranked drivers for the shop. The shop then assigns one of the drivers in a new event. During the third phase ("delivery process") events are created when the flowers are picked up by the driver and dropped off at the customer's location. In the fourth phase ("ranking evaluation") the system generates ranking increase and decrease events according to the delivery performance based on recent events. Phase five ("activity monitoring") aggregates driver's assignments and other events to create a monthly report on the quality of service per driver. Various alerts during the process are emitted as further events.

Modelling the scenario requires static data, events and streams. Examples of static data are the flower shops as well as drivers and location features like regions of delivery. For the regions we placed the delivery scenario in the city of Berlin and fetched the city quarters of Berlin from existing Linked Data. An example is given further below.

The following listing illustrates static data about drivers. An entity of type `Driver` is shown with a ranking of five. The listing uses RDF Turtle syntax:

```
@prefix owl: <http://www.w3.org/2002/07/owl#> .
@prefix rdf: <http://www.w3.org/1999/02/22-rdf-syntax-ns#> .
@prefix xsd: <http://www.w3.org/2001/XMLSchema#> .
@prefix :    <http://events.event-processing.org/ffd/> .

:John rdf:type :Driver ;
      :ranking "5"^^xsd:int .
```

For the geographical information about drivers, not only geo coordinates are used but also geographical names to allow more course-grained assignments to city regions in the scenario. To that end we crawled Linked

Data from DBpedia[4] about geographical names of the city quarters of Berlin in RDF. The advantage of using Linked Data here is that the entities are identified and modelled for re-use in RDF-oriented scenarios. The following listing illustrates the properties we used from the Berlin quarter of *Charlottenburg*:

```
@prefix dbpedia:  <http://dbpedia.org/resource/> .
@prefix dbpedia-owl:  <http://dbpedia.org/ontology/> .
@prefix dbpprop:  <http://dbpedia.org/property/> .

dbpedia:Charlottenburg
      rdf:type dbpedia-owl:PopulatedPlace , dbpedia-owl:Place , dbpedia
           -owl:Settlement , yago:LocalitiesOfBerlin ;
      dbpprop:area 10.6 ;
      dbpprop:city "Berlin"@en ;
      dbpprop:density 11198 ;
      dbpprop:name "Charlottenburg"@en ;
      dbpprop:population 118704 ;
      dbpprop:populationAsOf
              2008 ;
      dbpprop:type "Quarter"@en ;
      dbpprop:year 1705 ;
      geo:lat "52.5167"^^xsd:float ;
      geo:long "13.3"^^xsd:float ;
      ...
```

The next listing illustrates an entity of type `Shop` with a minimum ranking for viable drivers:

```
FlowerShop42
      rdf:type :Shop ;
      :minimumRanking "2"^^xsd:int .
```

Streams are defined in RDF according to our model (cf. Section 5.3) as follows:

```
ffd:AssignmentChannel
      rdf:type :Stream .

ffd:DeliveryRequestChannel
      rdf:type :Stream .

ffd:DriverLocationChannel
      rdf:type :Stream .
```

[4]DBpedia: http://dbpedia.org

We created an event hierarchy for the scenario as illustrated in Figure 8.7. According to our model the events are subclasses of class `Event`. Apart from the parent class the hierarchy is disjoint from event classes created for previous scenarios (e.g. in Figure 5.2). The classes in this scenario also are in a separate namespace, `ffd:`, so that they are uniquely identified and their schema may be administered independently from other schemas.

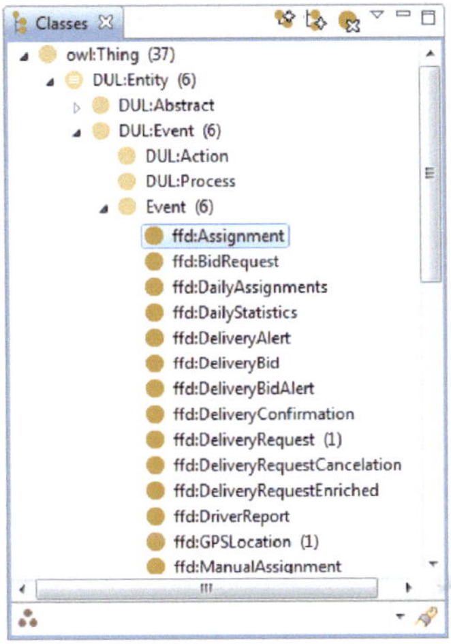

Figure 8.7.: Event Type Hierarchy for the Fast Flower Delivery Scenario

Listing 8.3 shows an event of type `DeliveryRequest` from the bid phase. The event illustrates our event model using timestamps defined in Section 5.3 as `startTime` and `endTime`. Linked Data is used to refer to further context of the event, e.g. the Berlin quarter mentioned above and the stream.

Our implementation of the Fast Flower Delivery scenario is available as open-source software[5], see also Appendix A.1. The implementation includes events, static data, event patterns and code to test the scenario.

[5]Fast Flower Delivery (FFD) Scenario: https://github.com/play-project/play-test/tree/develop/play-test-fast-flower-delivery

```
@prefix :       <http://events.event-processing.org/types/> .
@prefix ffd:    <http://events.event-processing.org/ffd/> .

<http://events.event-processing.org/ids/deliveryRequestEvent#event>
      rdf:type ffd:DeliveryRequest ;
      ffd:addresseeLocation
              <http://dbpedia.org/resource/Charlottenburg> ;
      ffd:requestId 128 ;
      ffd:requiredDeliveryTime
              "2014-03-18T20:00:01.011Z"^^xsd:dateTime ;
      ffd:requiredPickupTime
              "2014-03-18T12:42:01.011Z"^^xsd:dateTime ;
      ffd:store ffd:FlowerShop42 ;
      :stream ffd:DeliveryRequestChannel ;
      :endTime "2014-03-15T12:42:01.012Z"^^xsd:dateTime ;
      :startTime "2014-03-15T12:42:01.011Z"^^xsd:dateTime .
```

Listing 8.3: Linked Data for the Fast Flower Delivery Scenario

8.6. Discussion

We have evaluated our system in parts and in total, quantitatively and qualitatively, have compared it to the state of the art and have implemented an archetype scenario.

In conclusion, we have shown that each of the requirements is met. We have confirmed that our implementation ranks above average in the qualitative benchmark comparing the language expressivity of the state of the art in RDF event processing. Also, we have shown quantitatively what the cost is of using native RDF in event processing and confirming that our combined system scales satisfactorily.

9 Conclusions and Outlook

In this thesis we developed models, methods and an instantiation (system) to make the Web situation-aware. Our models describe a schema for events and a language to process events. Our methods describe protocols to exchange events on the Web, algorithms to execute the language and to calculate access rights. Finally, our system realises and integrates the previous contributions in a running implementation. We conclude this thesis by summing up the research questions, achieved results, drawing conclusions and providing an outlook on future work.

Based on the observation that an increasing volume of real-time data is available on the Web and that a technology is needed to make sense of these data we raised the principal research question in this thesis:

How can the Web be made situation-aware?

Event processing is a suitable technology for gaining real-time results. However, most existing related work in event processing is designed for closed-domain settings. It cannot trivially be applied to the Web. Thus, we collected requirements for event processing on the Web. Event processing generally uses three ingredients which we employed to structure our three research questions: events, processing languages and a system to evaluate the languages over events. Hence, for the use on the Web we raised the research questions: Research Question 1: (Web Interoperability) about events, Research Question 2: (Processing Language) and Research Question 3: (Infrastructure) about a system. In the following we describe the results achieved, answering each of the questions.

9.1. Summary of the Results

The first research question addresses a model for events with the goal of interoperability on the Web:

Research Question 1 (Web Interoperability). *How can we achieve event interoperability for situation awareness at a Web scale?*

We answered this question by designing an event model in RDF. First we collected requirements for an event model from related work, research literature, best practises for Web data modelling and Linked Data, scenarios such as the Real-time Web grand challenge, the vision of the event marketplace, a crisis management scenario and a telecommunications scenario described by domain experts. The requirements covered modelling events as first class objects, supporting temporal and geo-spatial properties, supporting type hierarchies and further relationships between events, the use of open standards and re-use of existing schemas to foster interoperability, satisfying the Linked Data guidelines, providing metadata for search and enabling adaptivity of the schema to address changing needs of users.

The second research question addresses the processing language to detect meaningful situations on the Web:

Research Question 2 (Processing Language). *How to design and realise a processing language for Web events?*

We answered this research question by designing an event processing language based on the RDF query language SPARQL. First we collected requirements from related work, research literature and our scenarios. The requirements covered matching the data model, supporting event-driven processing including temporal query operators, the ability to query both real-time and historic events, supporting the expressivity needed by our scenarios and employing open standards.

The third and final research question addresses the infrastructure to manage events and queries:

Research Question 3 (Infrastructure). *How to design and develop an efficient infrastructure supporting a Web of events?*

We answered this research question by designing and implementing an open source system to process events, execute our processing language, manage streams of events including metadata search and access rights and implement adapters and tools to re-use existing real-time event sources. First we collected requirements from related work, research literature, our scenarios, existing event sources and the vision of an event marketplace. The requirements for our system covered the parsing and understanding of event models, evaluating real-time and historic queries, processing events in real-time, the integration of existing event sources to realise our scenarios, Linked Data guidelines, employing open standards, supporting multitenancy by separating users by access control and by allowing them to add and remove event patterns dynamically at any time when users' needs change, and lastly by supporting programmers with programmable tools such as SDKs.

9.1.1. Event Model

Addressing Research Question 1: (Web Interoperability) and its requirements we presented our event model for RDF. The model is designed for the use on the Web with many users, and many application domains. Thus, the model enforces only a minimum set of event properties and leaves room for extensibility. We defined the set of mandatory properties to describe the core characteristics of an event and thus facilitate basic temporal event processing required by all of our scenarios. Furthermore, we defined optional properties to enable common but not mandatory use cases such as geographic filtering of events required by some of our scenarios. Moreover, the model was designed for extensibility. The schema language RDFS used in our modelling is multi-schema friendly and particularly well suited for re-use of schemas across the Web and at a fine-grained granularity allowing the re-use and mixing of multiple schemas. The mandatory time-oriented properties were chosen to support both point-based and interval-based events as needed by our scenarios.

9.1.2. Event Pattern Language

Addressing Research Question 2: (Processing Language) and its requirements we presented our event processing language BDPL. The language supports event-at-a-time operators to describe fine-grained situations where very specific events must be matched. Also the language supports set-at-a-time operators to detect coarse-grained situations where only aggregate values from sets of events are sufficient to find a match. Since real-time data in streams often need to be augmented with static background knowledge or historical data our language supports so-called hybrid queries which match both data from real-time streams and data from data stores. The language is designed as a variation of SPARQL, the well-known query language for RDF. As such the language is a good match for the underlying data representation in RDF and from a users' perspective the language is not completely new to learn.

9.1.3. Event Processing System

Addressing Research Question 3: (Infrastructure) and its requirements we presented our event processing system built on open standards. The system manages events in our open and extensible event model. Events are fed into the system using standards such as WS-Notification. The logic of the system is provided by expressions in our event pattern language based on SPARQL. Various types of tooling are supported by our system. The tools help modelling events programmatically, send and receive events to integrate new scenarios with our system, manage events by setting access rights and search for streams to be used in new scenarios. The system combines all of our contributions in one implemented stack of tools.

9.2. Significance of the Results

Our system employs event processing on the Web. Whereas event processing was previously only used in closed-domain applications, the focus on Web standards makes event processing feasible in an open setting. Data description in RDF and query languages like SPARQL have tried the same for static data. By employing re-usable schemas, RDF and SPARQL are gaining traction in the realisation of a Web of data. On the Web of data formal, structured queries can be posed against distributed datasets. For the integration of real-time streams such systems are not yet standardised. However, as this thesis showed, the same principles of data management can be applied.

In this thesis we answered the question of how to make the Web situation-aware by being able to fulfil structured queries over real-time, streaming data. To that end we designed and developed a Web-oriented event processing system. It uses Web-standards such as RDF, SPARQL and WS-Notification. The system combines open standards, self-descriptiveness and extensible schemas of RDF. Thus, this work addresses the requirements from the event processing challenge of a Real-time Web: distributed ownership and reach of the Web, the community-based, self-curated, constantly updated nature of Wikipedia as well as the adaptive nature of complex multitenant systems.

Our work can be used for the consolidation of real-time data from the Internet of Services (IoS) with data from the Internet of Things (IoT) and from the Social Web. This was achieved by designing and developing a general-purpose event processing engine with the open data description format RDF, thus enabling the combination of arbitrary data sources where each source retains the freedom and flexibility to create and extend its schemas. Especially the re-use and mashup of available schemas facilitates the combination of schemas from the IoS with schemas from the IoT (e.g. the W3C Semantic Sensor Network (SSN) Ontology) using spontaneous events emitted from either or both sources and combined in real-time using our work.

Our system was designed with two purpose-built components, one for event processing and one for storage. Our language interpreter can then compute queries over both of them and produce combined results. According to the book [Marz and Warren 2015] Lambda Architecture is an upcoming design principle to build such architectures. The "speed layer" from the Lambda Architecture corresponds with our real-time and stream management component DCEP, whereas the "batch layer" corresponds with our storage component. The "serving layer" from the Lambda Architecture is responsible for correlation of results from both previous layers, represented in our work by our unified, hybrid query language. Our design is thus well in line with the state of the art in system architecture even before the term Lambda Architecture was coined.

9.3. Outlook

Future work can be seen going in at least two directions: performance and expressivity.

Parsing of RDF is a large part of the computational work necessary when an event is received in our components. This is a shortcoming of text-based data representations like RDF but also XML. However, performance optimizations for RDF exist much like for XML. Examples are binary on-the-wire representations which are less verbose. Another example is JSON which is a very concise text-based representation. It does not allow complex datatypes or schemas, but the JSON-LD[1] specification provides a mapping to and from RDF so that semantics can be maintained. These data representations can be evaluated during further optimisation and re-evaluation of our work.

Another performance bottleneck was the communication of our components in Java with the underlying event processing engine written in Prolog. Using such different native language interpreters or virtual machines, the data (i.e. events) cannot easily flow between the two. The inter-process communication between Java and Prolog must be optimised. A way out of this problem is the replacement of the Prolog event processing engine with a pure-Java engine. That way no communication between Java and a different interpreter is necessary. However, a matching event processing engine must be found which can deal with RDF and fulfil all requirements stated in this work.

Distributed event processing must also be researched for increasing throughput and thus processing events using Web technologies at Web scale. A lot of related work such as [Xing et al. 2005] already exists and must be evaluated for its application with RDF data. Our work is prepared for parallel execution by employing frameworks such as ProActive. Event processing in general is a good candidate for horizontal scaling because of the immutability of events which greatly reduces the data dependencies of components. As such distributed event processing is a natural next step.

In terms of expressivity some use cases required the processing of continuous, numerical data such as the radiation increase in the nuclear crisis scenario. However, event processing languages (ours being no exception) are designed for discrete processing of events. Thus, numerical processing of continuous data is an interesting field for extending event processing. More scenarios can be covered when adding language features covering continuous data such as curves of radiation measurements, ECG time series from wearable cardio sensors (continuously providing 256 values per second) or geographical paths (e.g. series of points). Such scenarios need different abstractions to write short and concise queries, e.g. to find

[1] JSON for Linking Data: http://json-ld.org/

specific shapes in a curve of real-time sensor data or use statistical methods on such data.

Another important direction for future research should be the usability of query authoring. Non-technical users today can easily query the Web by writing keyword queries. However, the Real-time Web supports e.g. temporal relatedness of events which must be expressed explicitly by the use of temporal query operators. Such operators must be learned and correctly applied by users. A lot of work has been conducted in the field of graphical user interfaces for query design [Sen et al. 2009] and in the field of natural language interfaces [Linehan et al. 2011]. The former enable a user to draw a query graph on a canvas using events and event operators whereas the latter enable a user to write short sentences in a simplified natural language using a controlled vocabulary of temporal operators and event properties. Both attempts are promising but have not seen widespread adoption by non-technical users so far. Making the Real-time Web user-friendly still needs further work.

Appendix

A
Open-source Contributions

This appendix lists the contributions we made to free and open-source software. First, we describe where to find the sources for this work and in a second section we describe where to find pre-compiled binary artefacts.

A.1. Source Code

The results of our work are published open-source. This includes the designed artefacts such as our models and software components described above in Chapters 5 to 7 but also experimental data and test programmes to reproduce our evaluation results described in Chapter 8.

We publish our components under a free open-source license providing users the rights to re-use our approach and study, change and distribute the software to anyone and for any purpose [Laurent 2008]. Furthermore,

Table A.1.: Source Code Locations on the Web

Component	Source Code (https://github.com/...)
Event Model and its SDK	play-project/play-commons/
DCEP	play-project/play-dcep/
Access Control	play-project/play-commons/tree/master/play-commons-accesscontrol
Event Adapters for Twitter, Facebook and Xively events	play-project/play-eventadapters/
WebApp	play-project/WebApp/
Experimental datasets and benchmarks	play-project/play-test/

we publish our experimental datasets and test setup to enable users to reproduce our evaluation results. Additional technical documentation such as an install guide[1] and a developers guide[2] are provided.

Table A.1 shows the location of the artefact sources. Related components developed by third parties are also made available open-source by those parties. Such components include the service bus *DSB*[3], the storage component *EventCloud*[4] and the *Governance*[5] component. The RDF framework *RDFReactor*[6] is also available on the Web. It is used as underpinnings to our event modelling SDK and we contributed to it.

[1]Install Guide: https://github.com/play-project/play-dcep/tree/develop/play-dcep-distribution-etalis/README.md

[2]Developers Guide: https://github.com/play-project/play-dcep/blob/develop/README.eclipse.md

[3]DSB Code on Github: PetalsLinkLabs/petals-dsb/

[4]EventCloud Code: http://eventcloud.inria.fr/

[5]Governance Code on Github: play-project/play-governance/

[6]RDFReactor Code: http://code.google.com/p/semweb4j/

A.2. Binary Artefacts

To make re-use of our software easier for developers, pre-compiled binaries are available on the Web. All artefacts compiled from our code are published using Maven[7] repositories. Consequently, developers can create tools incorporating our technology using Maven, automating the process of resolving and downloading all required dependencies.

Figure A.1 shows the components of our contribution Distributed Complex Event Processing (DCEP).

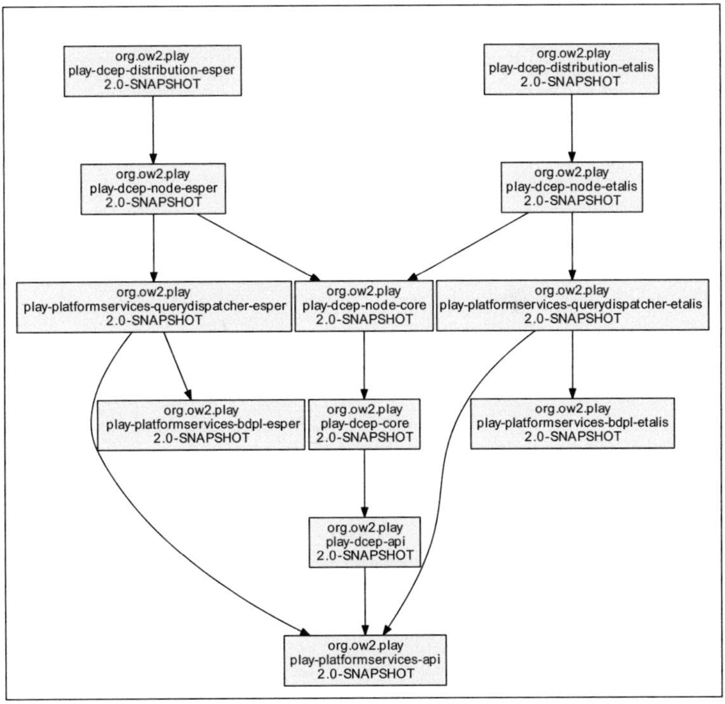

Figure A.1.: Module Interdependencies of all DCEP Software Artefacts

[7]Maven Build Tool: http://maven.apache.org/

A.3. Grammar

Our language BDPL is a derivation from SPARQL 1.1 as explained in Section 6.3. Thus, we modified a grammar of SPARQL to obtain a grammar for our language. The Jena ARQ[8] library contains such a grammar.

We modified the grammar from Jena ARQ and stored our result together with our other open-source contributions at the following address:

https://github.com/play-project/play-dcep

The grammar is available as an input file for the parser generator JavaCC[9] and as online documentation in HTML form.

[8] ARQ – A SPARQL Processor for Jena: http://jena.apache.org/documentation/query/
[9] JavaCC – The Java Parser Generator: https://javacc.java.net/

B Listings

This appendix contains the full listings of event patterns used in the evaluation in Section 8.4.

B.1. Overall System Test

The patterns in BDPL match four events of different types where the subsequent patterns add complexity in (i) testing for event content and (ii) including historic data.

The patterns are part of the experimental setup described in the previous appendix and can be obtained from the Web address mentioned there.

The first pattern was chosen to stress-test the temporal matching of the event processing engine. The second pattern was chosen to test the content-based filtering capabilities and the third pattern adding historic data was chosen to test the retrieval of distributed static data and performing efficient joins.

```
#
# Basic pattern detecting 4 company-related events in sequence bounded
    by a time window.
#

PREFIX rdf:      <http://www.w3.org/1999/02/22-rdf-syntax-ns#>
PREFIX uctelco: <http://events.event-processing.org/uc/telco/>
PREFIX geo:      <http://www.w3.org/2003/01/geo/wgs84_pos#>
PREFIX xsd:      <http://www.w3.org/2001/XMLSchema#>
PREFIX :         <http://events.event-processing.org/types/>

CONSTRUCT {
  :e rdf:type :UcTelcoEsrRecom .
  :e :stream <http://streams.event-processing.org/ids/OverallResults01#
      stream> .
  :e uctelco:ackRequired "false"^^xsd:boolean .
  :e uctelco:answerRequired "false"^^xsd:boolean .
  :e :message "Pattern 01: Four tweets about our companies were
      detected."^^xsd:string .
  :e uctelco:action <blank://action1> .
  <blank://action1> rdf:type uctelco:OpenTwitter ;
    :screenName ?screenName01 .
  :e :members ?e1 , ?e2 , ?e3 , ?e4 .
}
WHERE {
  WINDOW {
    EVENT ?id1 {
      ?e1 rdf:type :google .
      ?e1 :stream <http://streams.event-processing.org/ids/TwitterFeed#
          stream> .
      ?e1 :screenName ?screenName01 .
      }
    SEQ
    EVENT ?id2 {
      ?e2 rdf:type :apple .
      ?e2 :stream <http://streams.event-processing.org/ids/TwitterFeed#
          stream> .
      }
    SEQ
    EVENT ?id3 {
      ?e3 rdf:type :microsoft .
      ?e3 :stream <http://streams.event-processing.org/ids/TwitterFeed#
          stream> .
      }
    SEQ
    EVENT ?id4 {
```

```
      ?e4 rdf:type :yahoo .
      ?e4 :stream <http://streams.event-processing.org/ids/TwitterFeed#stream> .
      }
  } ("PT5S"^^xsd:duration, sliding)
}
```

Listing B.1: Scenario-based Test: First Pattern (BDPL Syntax)

```
#
# Selective pattern detecting 4 company-related events in sequence bounded by a time window
# and filtering twitter events for number of friends and more.
#

PREFIX rdf:     <http://www.w3.org/1999/02/22-rdf-syntax-ns#>
PREFIX uctelco: <http://events.event-processing.org/uc/telco/>
PREFIX geo:     <http://www.w3.org/2003/01/geo/wgs84_pos#>
PREFIX xsd:     <http://www.w3.org/2001/XMLSchema#>
PREFIX :        <http://events.event-processing.org/types/>

CONSTRUCT {
  :e rdf:type :UcTelcoEsrRecom .
  :e :stream <http://streams.event-processing.org/ids/OverallResults02#stream> .
  :e uctelco:ackRequired "false"^^xsd:boolean .
  :e uctelco:answerRequired "false"^^xsd:boolean .
  :e :message "Pattern 02: Four company-related events were detected using stricter filters."^^xsd:string .
  :e uctelco:action <blank://action1> .
  <blank://action1> rdf:type uctelco:OpenTwitter ;
    :screenName ?screenName01 .
  :e :members ?e1 , ?e2 , ?e3 , ?e4 .
}
WHERE {
  WINDOW {
    EVENT ?id1 {
      ?e1 rdf:type :google .
      ?e1 :stream <http://streams.event-processing.org/ids/TwitterFeed#stream> .
      ?e1 :screenName ?screenName01 .
      ?e1 :isRetweet "false" .
      ?e1 :friendsCount ?friendsCount01 .
      }
      FILTER(?friendsCount01 > "10")
    SEQ
    EVENT ?id2 {
      ?e2 rdf:type :apple .
      ?e2 :stream <http://streams.event-processing.org/ids/TwitterFeed#stream> .
      ?e2 :isRetweet "false" .
      ?e2 :friendsCount ?friendsCount02 .
      }
```

```
      FILTER(?friendsCount02 > "10")
    SEQ
    EVENT ?id3 {
      ?e3 rdf:type :microsoft .
      ?e3 :stream <http://streams.event-processing.org/ids/TwitterFeed#
          stream> .
      ?e3 :isRetweet "false" .
      ?e3 :friendsCount ?friendsCount03 .
      }
      FILTER(?friendsCount03 > "10")
    SEQ
    EVENT ?id4 {
      ?e4 rdf:type :yahoo .
      ?e4 :stream <http://streams.event-processing.org/ids/TwitterFeed#
          stream> .
      ?e4 :isRetweet "false" .
      ?e4 :friendsCount ?friendsCount04 .
      }
      FILTER(?friendsCount04 > "10")
  } ("PT5S"^^xsd:duration, sliding)
}
```

Listing B.2: Scenario-based Test: Second Pattern (BDPL Syntax)

```
#
# Real-time and historic pattern detecting 4 company-related events
     where one poster has previously posted in the past.
#

PREFIX rdf:      <http://www.w3.org/1999/02/22-rdf-syntax-ns#>
PREFIX uctelco: <http://events.event-processing.org/uc/telco/>
PREFIX geo:      <http://www.w3.org/2003/01/geo/wgs84_pos#>
PREFIX xsd:      <http://www.w3.org/2001/XMLSchema#>
PREFIX :         <http://events.event-processing.org/types/>

CONSTRUCT {
  :e rdf:type :UcTelcoEsrRecom .
  :e :stream <http://streams.event-processing.org/ids/OverallResults03#
      stream> .
  :e uctelco:ackRequired "false"^^xsd:boolean .
  :e uctelco:answerRequired "false"^^xsd:boolean .
  :e :message "Pattern 03: Four company-related events were detected
      where one poster has previously posted in the past."^^xsd:string
      .
  :e uctelco:action <blank://action1> .
  <blank://action1> rdf:type uctelco:OpenTwitter ;
    :screenName ?screenName01 .
  :e :members ?e1 , ?e2 , ?e3 , ?e4 .
}
WHERE {
  WINDOW {
    EVENT ?id1 {
      ?e1 rdf:type :google .
```

```
      ?e1 :stream <http://streams.event-processing.org/ids/TwitterFeed#
           stream> .
      ?e1 :screenName ?screenName01 .
      }
    SEQ
    EVENT ?id2 {
      ?e2 rdf:type :apple .
      ?e2 :stream <http://streams.event-processing.org/ids/TwitterFeed#
           stream> .
      ?e2 :screenName ?screenName02 .
      }
    SEQ
    EVENT ?id3 {
      ?e3 rdf:type :microsoft .
      ?e3 :stream <http://streams.event-processing.org/ids/TwitterFeed#
           stream> .
      }
    SEQ
    EVENT ?id4 {
      ?e4 rdf:type :yahoo .
      ?e4 :stream <http://streams.event-processing.org/ids/TwitterFeed#
           stream> .
      }
  } ("PT5S"^^xsd:duration, sliding)
  GRAPH ?id5 {
    ?e5 :stream <http://streams.event-processing.org/ids/TwitterFeed#
         stream> .
    ?e5 :screenName ?screenName02 .
  }
}
```

Listing B.3: Scenario-based Test: Third Pattern (BDPL Syntax)

Bibliography

Adi, Asaf; Botzer, David; Etzion, Opher (2000). 'Semantic Event Model and its Implication on Situation Detection'. In: *ECIS*. Wirtschaftsuniversität Wien (WU).

Aguilera, Marcos K.; Strom, Robert E.; Sturman, Daniel C.; Astley, Mark; Chandra, Tushar D. (1999). 'Matching events in a content-based subscription system'. In: *PODC '99: Proceedings of the eighteenth annual ACM Symposium on Principles of Distributed Computing*. New York, NY, USA: ACM, pp. 53–61. ISBN: 1-58113-099-6. DOI: 10.1145/301308.301326.

Allen, James F. (1981). 'An interval based representation of temporal knowledge'. In: *In Proc. of the 7 IJCAI*, pp. 221–226.

Aničić, Darko (2012). *Event Processing and Stream Reasoning with ETALIS*. Saarbrücken: Südwestdeutscher Verlag für Hochschulschriften. ISBN: 9783838131733.

Anicic, Darko; Fodor, Paul; Stühmer, Roland; Stojanovic, Nenad (2009). 'Event-driven Approach for Logic-based Complex Event Processing'. In: *CSE '09: Proceedings of the 2009 12th IEEE International Conference on Computational Science and Engineering*. Washington, DC, USA: IEEE Computer Society.

Barbieri, Davide Francesco; Braga, Daniele; Ceri, Stefano; Valle, Emanuele Della; Grossniklaus, Michael (2010). 'Querying RDF streams with C-SPARQL'. In: *SIGMOD Rec.* 39.1, pp. 20–26. ISSN: 0163-5808. DOI: 10.1145/1860702.1860705.

Barthe-Delanoë, Anne-Marie; Truptil, Sebastien; Stühmer, Roland; Benaben, Frederick (2012). 'Definition of a Nuclear Crisis Use-case Management to S(t)imulate an Event Management Platform'. In: *7th International Workshop on Semantic Business Process Management (SBPM 2012)*. Vol. 862. CEUR Workshop Proceedings. SBPM Workshop, pp. 128–137.

Benaben, Frederick; Gibert, Philippe; Stühmer, Roland (2013). *PLAY Deliverable D6.3.6 – Evaluation Report concerning the two Use Cases' Execution on the PLAY Platform*. Project Deliverable. PLAY Collaborative Project 258659.

Berners-Lee, Tim (2005). *What HTTP URIs Identify? – Design Issues*. Online Article. http://www.w3.org/DesignIssues/HTTP-URI2.html Last accessed 2014-05-02.

Berners-Lee, Tim (2006). *Linked Data*. http://www.w3.org/DesignIssues/LinkedData.html Last accessed 2014-05-02.

Berners-Lee, Tim (2009). *WebAccessControl*. Online resource. http://www.w3.org/wiki/WebAccessControl Last accessed 2014-05-02.

Berrueta, Diego (2010). *SIOC Core Ontology Specification*. Online resource. http://rdfs.org/sioc/spec/ Last accessed 2014-05-02.

Bizer, Chris; Cyganiak, Richard (2014). *RDF 1.1 TriG*. W3C Recommendation. http://www.w3.org/TR/trig/ Last accessed 2014-05-02.

Brickley, Dan (2003). *Basic Geo (WGS84 lat/long) Vocabulary*. Online Article. W3C Semantic Web Interest Group. http://www.w3.org/2003/01/geo/ Last updated 2004. Last accessed 2014-05-02.

Bry, F.; Eckert, M. (2006). 'Twelve theses on reactive rules for the web'. In: *Proceedings of the Workshop on Reactivity on the Web, Munich, Germany*.

Calbimonte, Jean-Paul; Corcho, Oscar; Gray, Alasdair J.G. (2010). 'Enabling Ontology-Based Access to Streaming Data Sources'. In: *The Semantic Web – ISWC 2010*. Ed. by Peter F. Patel-Schneider; Yue Pan; Pascal Hitzler; Peter Mika; Lei Zhang; Jeff Z. Pan; Ian Horrocks; Birte Glimm. Vol. 6496. Lecture Notes in Computer Science. Springer Berlin Heidelberg, pp. 96–111. ISBN: 978-3-642-17745-3. DOI: 10.1007/978-3-642-17746-0_7.

Cardelli, Luca (2004). 'Type Systems'. In: *CRC Handbook of Computer Science and Engineering*. Ed. by Allen Tucker. Boca Raton, Fla: CRC Press. Chap. 97, pp. 97/1–97/32. ISBN: 158488360X.

Carzaniga, Antonio; Rosenblum, David S.; Wolf, Alexander L. (2001). 'Design and evaluation of a wide-area event notification service'. In: *ACM*

Trans. Comput. Syst. 19.3, pp. 332–383. ISSN: 0734-2071. DOI: 10.1145/380749.380767.

Chandy, Mani K.; Etzion, Opher; Ammon, Rainer von (2011). '10201 Executive Summary and Manifesto – Event Processing'. In: *Event Processing*. Ed. by K. Mani Chandy; Opher Etzion; Rainer von Ammon. Dagstuhl Seminar Proceedings 10201. Dagstuhl, Germany: Schloss Dagstuhl - Leibniz-Zentrum fuer Informatik, Germany.

Dindar, Nihal; Fischer, Peter M.; Soner, Merve; Tatbul, Nesime (2011). 'Efficiently correlating complex events over live and archived data streams'. In: *Proceedings of the 5th ACM International Conference on Distributed Event-Based Systems*. Ed. by David M. Eyers; Opher Etzion; Avigdor Gal; Stanley B. Zdonik; Paul Vincent. ACM, pp. 243–254. ISBN: 978-1-4503-0423-8. DOI: 10.1145/2002259.2002293.

Endsley, M.R.; Garland, D.J. (2000). *Situation Awareness Analysis and Measurement*. Taylor & Francis. ISBN: 9781410605306.

Etzion, Opher; Niblett, Peter (2010). *Event Processing in Action*. Manning Publications Co. ISBN: 978-1935182214.

Fidler, E.; Jacobsen, H.-A.; Li, G.; Mankovski, S. (2005). 'The Padres distributed publish/subscribe System'. In: *In 8th International Conference on Feature Interactions in Telecommunications and Software Systems*, pp. 12–30.

Fielding, R.; Gettys, J.; Mogul, J.; Frystyk, H.; Masinter, L.; Leach, P.; Berners-Lee, T. (1999). *Hypertext Transfer Protocol – HTTP/1.1*. RFC. United States.

Filali, Imen; Pellegrino, Laurent; Bongiovanni, Francesco; Huet, Fabrice; Baude, Françoise (2011). 'Modular P2P-based Approach for RDF Data Storage and Retrieval'. In: *Proceedings of The Third International Conference on Advances in P2P Systems (AP2PS 2011)*.

Fromm, Ken (2009). *The Real-Time Web: A Primer*. Online Resource. http://readwrite.com/2009/08/29/the_real-time_web_a_primer_part_1 Last visited 2014-05-02.

Galton, Antony; Augusto, Juan Carlos (2002). 'Two Approaches to Event Definition'. In: *DEXA '02: Proceedings of the 13th International Conference on Database and Expert Systems Applications*. London, UK: Springer-Verlag, pp. 547–556. ISBN: 3-540-44126-3.

Gangemi, Aldo; Guarino, Nicola; Masolo, Claudio; Oltramari, Alessandro; Schneider, Luc (2002). 'Sweetening Ontologies with DOLCE'. In:

Proceedings of the 13th International Conference on Knowledge Engineering and Knowledge Management. Ontologies and the Semantic Web. EKAW '02. London, UK: Springer-Verlag, pp. 166–181. ISBN: 3-540-44268-5.

Garrett, Jesse James (2005). *Ajax: A New Approach to Web Applications*. Online article. http://www.adaptivepath.com/ideas/ajax-new-approach-web-applications/. Last visited: 2014-05-02.

Gupta, Amarnath; Jain, Ramesh (2011). *Managing Event Information: Modeling, Retrieval, and Applications*. 1st. Synthesis Lectures on Data Management. Morgan & Claypool Publishers. ISBN: 1608453510, 9781608453511. DOI: 10.2200/S00374ED1V01Y201107DTM019.

Gutierrez, Claudio; Hurtado, Carlos A.; Vaisman, Alejandro (2007). 'Introducing Time into RDF'. In: *IEEE Transactions on Knowledge and Data Engineering* 19, pp. 207–218. ISSN: 1041-4347. DOI: 10.1109/TKDE.2007.34.

Harris, Steve; Seaborne, Andy (2010). *SPARQL 1.1 Query Language*. W3C Recommendation. http://www.w3.org/TR/sparql11-query/ Last accessed 2014-05-02.

Harth, Andreas; Stühmer, Roland (2011). *Publishing Event Streams as Linked Data*. Online Article. http://km.aifb.kit.edu/sites/lodstream/ Last visited 2014-05-02. Karlsruhe Institute of Technology, FZI Forschungszentrum Informatik.

Hevner, A. R.; March, S. T.; Park, J.; Ram, S. (2004). 'Design Science in Information Systems Research'. In: *MIS Quarterly* 28.1, pp. 75–106.

Jain, Ramesh (2007). 'Toward EventWeb'. In: *IEEE Distributed Systems Online* 8.9. ISSN: 1541-4922. DOI: 10.1109/MDSO.2007.56.

Klyne, Graham; Carroll, Jeremy J. (2004). *Resource Description Framework (RDF): Concepts and Abstract Syntax*. W3C Recommendation. http://www.w3.org/TR/rdf-concepts/ Last accessed 2014-05-02.

Komazec, Srdjan; Cerri, Davide; Fensel, Dieter (2012). 'Sparkwave: Continuous Schema-enhanced Pattern Matching over RDF Data Streams'. In: *Proceedings of the 6th ACM International Conference on Distributed Event-Based Systems*. DEBS '12. New York, NY, USA: ACM, pp. 58–68. ISBN: 978-1-4503-1315-5. DOI: 10.1145/2335484.2335491.

Kreger, Heather (2005). *OASIS Web Services Distributed Management (WSDM) TC*. Online Resource. http://www.oasis-open.org/committees/tc_home.php?wg_abbrev=wsdm.

Lauras, Matthieu; Stühmer, Roland; Verginadis, Yiannis; Benaben, Frederick (2012). 'An event-driven platform to manage agility'. In: *Proceedings of the 6th IEEE Int. Conf. on Digital Ecosystems and Technologies for Complex Systems, Environment, and Service Engineering IEEE-DEST 2012.*

Laurent, Andrew St. (2008). *Understanding Open Source and Free Software Licensing*. Sebastopol: O'Reilly Media, Inc. ISBN: 9780596553951.

Linehan, Mark H.; Dehors, Sylvain; Rabinovich, Ella; Fournier, Fabiana (2011). 'Controlled English Language for Production and Event Processing Rules'. In: *Proceedings of the 5th ACM International Conference on Distributed Event-based System*. DEBS '11. New York, New York, USA: ACM, pp. 149–158. ISBN: 978-1-4503-0423-8. DOI: 10.1145/2002259.2002281.

Luckham, David C. (2001). *The Power of Events: An Introduction to Complex Event Processing in Distributed Enterprise Systems*. Boston, MA, USA: Addison-Wesley Longman Publishing Co., Inc. ISBN: 0201727897.

Luckham, David C.; Schulte, Roy (2011). *Event Processing Glossary - Version 2.0*. Online Resource. http://www.complexevents.com/2011/08/23/event-processing-glossary-version-2-0/ Last visited 2014-05-02.

Maier, David; Li, Jin; Tucker, Peter; Tufte, Kristin; Papadimos, Vassilis (2005). 'Semantics of Data Streams and Operators'. In: *Proceedings of the 10th International Conference on Database Theory*. ICDT'05. Edinburgh, UK: Springer-Verlag, pp. 37–52. ISBN: 3-540-24288-0, 978-3-540-24288-8. DOI: 10.1007/978-3-540-30570-5_3.

Martin-Flatin, J.P. (1999). 'Push vs. pull in Web-based network management'. In: *Integrated Network Management, 1999. Distributed Management for the Networked Millennium. Proceedings of the Sixth IFIP/IEEE International Symposium on*, pp. 3–18. DOI: 10.1109/INM.1999.770671.

Marz, Nathan; Warren, James (2015). *Big Data: Principles and Best Practices of Scalable Realtime Data Systems*. Early Access Edition, final book to appear in 2015. Manning Publications Co. ISBN: 9781617290343.

Mühl, Gero; Fiege, Ludger; Pietzuch, Peter (2006). *Distributed Event-Based Systems*. Secaucus, NJ, USA: Springer-Verlag New York, Inc. ISBN: 3-540-32651-0.

Norton, Barry; Krummenacher, Reto (2010). 'Consuming Dynamic Linked Data'. In: *Proceedings of the First International Workshop on Consuming Linked Data (COLD2010)*. Ed. by Olaf Hartig; Andreas Harth; Juan Sequeda. Vol. 665. CEUR Workshop Proceedings. COLD Workshop.

Noy, Natasha; Rector, Alan (2006). *Defining N-ary Relations on the Semantic Web*. W3C Working Group Note. World Wide Web Consortium.

Ostrowski, Krzysztof; Birman, Ken; Dolev, Danny (2007). 'Live Distributed Objects: Enabling the Active Web'. In: *IEEE Internet Computing* 11.6, pp. 72–78. ISSN: 1089-7801. DOI: 10.1109/MIC.2007.131.

Pellegrino, Laurent; Huet, Fabrice; Baude, Françoise; Alshabani, Amjad (2013). 'A Distributed Publish/Subscribe System for RDF Data'. In: *Data Management in Cloud, Grid and P2P Systems*. Springer, pp. 39–50.

Pérez, Jorge; Arenas, Marcelo; Gutierrez, Claudio (2009). 'Semantics and complexity of SPARQL'. In: *ACM Trans. Database Syst.* 34.3, 16:1–16:45. ISSN: 0362-5915. DOI: 10.1145/1567274.1567278.

Petrovic, Milenko; Liu, Haifeng; Jacobsen, Hans-Arno (2005). 'G-ToPSS: Fast Filtering of graph-based Metadata'. In: *WWW '05: Proceedings of the 14th International Conference on World Wide Web*. New York, NY, USA: ACM, pp. 539–547. ISBN: 1-59593-046-9. DOI: 10.1145/1060745.1060824.

Le-Phuoc, Danh; Dao-Tran, Minh; Parreira, Josiane Xavier; Hauswirth, Manfred (2011). 'A native and adaptive approach for unified processing of linked streams and linked data'. In: *Proceedings of the 10th international conference on The semantic web - Volume Part I*. ISWC'11. Berlin, Heidelberg: Springer-Verlag, pp. 370–388. ISBN: 978-3-642-25072-9.

Pietzuch, Peter R.; Bacon, Jean M. (2002). 'Hermes: A Distributed Event-Based Middleware Architecture'. In: *ICDCSW '02: Proceedings of the 22nd International Conference on Distributed Computing Systems*. Washington, DC, USA: IEEE Computer Society, pp. 611–618. ISBN: 0-7695-1588-6.

Pinto, H. Sofia; Martins, J. P. (2000). 'Reusing Ontologies'. In: *In AAAI 2000 Spring Symposium on Bringing Knowledge to Business Processes*. AAAI Press, pp. 77–84.

Qian, Jianfeng; Yin, Jianwei; Shi, Dongcai; Dong, Jinxiang (2008). 'Exploring a Semantic Publish/Subscribe Middleware for Event-Based SOA'. In: *APSCC '08: Proceedings of the 2008 IEEE Asia-Pacific Services Computing Conference*. Washington, DC, USA: IEEE Computer Society, pp. 1269–1275. ISBN: 978-0-7695-3473-2. DOI: 10.1109/APSCC.2008.153.

Rinne, Mikko; Abdullah, Haris; Törmä, Seppo; Nuutila, Esko (2012). 'Processing Heterogeneous RDF Events with Standing SPARQL Update Rules'. In: *OTM Conferences (2)*. Ed. by Robert Meersman; Hervé Panetto; Tharam S. Dillon; Stefanie Rinderle-Ma; Peter Dadam; Xiaofang Zhou;

Siani Pearson; Alois Ferscha; Sonia Bergamaschi; Isabel F. Cruz. Vol. 7566. Lecture Notes in Computer Science. Springer, pp. 797–806. ISBN: 978-3-642-33614-0, 978-3-642-33615-7. DOI: 10.1007/978-3-642-33615-7_24.

Rinne, Mikko; Blomqvist, Eva; Keskisärkkä, Robin; Nuutila, Esko (2013). 'Event Processing in RDF'. In: *4th Workshop on Ontology and Semantic Web Patterns (WOP2013)*. CEUR Workshop Proceedings.

Rozsnyai, S.; Vecera, R.; Schiefer, J.; Schatten, A. (2007a). 'Event Cloud - Searching for Correlated Business Events'. In: *E-Commerce Technology and the 4th IEEE International Conference on Enterprise Computing, E-Commerce, and E-Services, 2007. CEC/EEE 2007. The 9th IEEE International Conference on*, pp. 409–420. DOI: 10.1109/CEC-EEE.2007.47.

Rozsnyai, Szabolcs; Schiefer, Josef; Schatten, Alexander (2007b). 'Concepts and models for typing events for event-based systems'. In: *Proceedings of the 1st ACM International Conference on Distributed Event-Based Systems*. New York, NY, USA: ACM, pp. 62–70. ISBN: 978-1-59593-665-3. DOI: 10.1145/1266894.1266904.

Russell, Alex (2006). *Comet: Low Latency Data for the Browser*. Online Article. http://infrequently.org/2006/03/comet-low-latency-data-for-the-browser/. Last visited: 2014-05-02.

Scherp, Ansgar; Franz, Thomas; Saathoff, Carsten; Staab, Steffen (2009). 'F–a Model of Events based on the foundational Ontology Dolce+DnS Ultralight'. In: *Proceedings of the fifth International Conference on Knowledge Capture*. K-CAP '09. New York, NY, USA: ACM, pp. 137–144. ISBN: 978-1-60558-658-8. DOI: 10.1145/1597735.1597760.

Schmidt, Kay-Uwe; Stühmer, Roland; Stojanovic, Ljiljana (2008). 'Blending Complex Event Processing with the RETE Algorithm'. In: *Proc. of iCEP2008: 1st International workshop on Complex Event Processing for the Future Internet colocated with the Future Internet Symposium (FIS2008)*. Ed. by Darko Anicic; Christian Brelage; Opher Etzion; Nenad Stojanovic. Vol. 412. CEUR Workshop Proceedings (CEUR-WS.org, ISSN 1613-0073).

Sen, Sinan; Stojanovic, Nenad (2010). 'GRUVe: A Methodology for Complex Event Pattern Life Cycle Management'. In: *Advanced Information Systems Engineering*. Ed. by Barbara Pernici. Vol. 6051. Lecture Notes in Computer Science. Springer Berlin / Heidelberg, pp. 209–223. DOI: {10.1007/978-3-642-13094-6_17}.

Sen, Sinan; Stojanovic, Nenad; Lin, Ruofeng (2009). 'A graphical editor for complex event pattern generation'. In: *Proceedings of the 3rd ACM International Conference on Distributed Event-Based Systems*. New York, NY, USA: ACM, pp. 1–2. ISBN: 978-1-60558-665-6. DOI: 10.1145/1619258.1619309.

Shaw, Ryan; Troncy, Raphael; Hardman, Lynda (2009). 'LODE: Linking Open Descriptions of Events'. In: *The Semantic Web*. Vol. 5926. Lecture Notes in Computer Science. Springer Berlin / Heidelberg, pp. 153–167. ISBN: 978-3-642-10870-9. DOI: 10.1007/978-3-642-10871-6_11.

Stadtmüller, Steffen; Speiser, Sebastian; Harth, Andreas; Studer, Rudi (2013). 'Data-Fu: A Language and an Interpreter for Interaction with Read/Write Linked Data'. In: *Proceedings of the 22nd International Conference on World Wide Web*. Republic and Canton of Geneva, Switzerland: International World Wide Web Conferences Steering Committee, pp. 1225–1236.

Stojanovic, Nenad; Stojanovic, Ljiljana; Anicic, Darko; Ma, Jun; Sen, Sinan; Stühmer, Roland (2011). 'Semantic Complex Event Reasoning – Beyond Complex Event Processing'. In: *Foundations for the Web of Information and Services*. Ed. by Dieter Fensel. Springer Berlin Heidelberg, pp. 253–279. ISBN: 978-3-642-19797-0. DOI: 10.1007/978-3-642-19797-0_14.

Stojanovic, Nenad; Stojanovic, Ljiljana; Stühmer, Roland (2013). 'Tutorial: Personal Big Data Management in Cyber-physical Systems – The Role of Event Processing'. In: *Proceedings of the 7th ACM international conference on Distributed event-based systems*. New York, NY, USA. ISBN: 978-1-4503-1758-0. DOI: 10.1145/2488222.2488348.

Stojanovic, Nenad; Stühmer, Roland; Gibert, Philippe; Baude, Françoise (2012). 'Tutorial: Where Event Processing Grand Challenge meets Real-time Web: PLAY Event Marketplace'. In: *Proceedings of the 6th ACM International Conference on Distributed Event-Based Systems*. Berlin, Germany: ACM, pp. 341–352. ISBN: 978-1-4503-1315-5. DOI: 10.1145/2335484.2335521.

Studer, Rudi; Benjamins, V. Richard; Fensel, Dieter (1998). 'Knowledge engineering: Principles and methods'. In: *Data & Knowledge Engineering* 25.1–2, pp. 161–197. ISSN: 0169-023X. DOI: 10.1016/S0169-023X(97)00056-6.

Stühmer, Roland; Anicic, Darko; Sen, Sinan; Ma, Jun; Schmidt, Kay-Uwe; Stojanovic, Nenad (2009a). 'Client-side Event Processing for Personalized Web Advertisement'. In: *On the Move to Meaningful Internet Systems: OTM 2009*. Vol. 5871. Lecture Notes in Computer Science. Springer Berlin / Heidelberg, pp. 1069–1086. ISBN: 978-3-642-05150-0. DOI: 10.1007/978-3-642-05151-7_23.

Stühmer, Roland; Anicic, Darko; Sen, Sinan; Ma, Jun; Schmidt, Kay-Uwe; Stojanovic, Nenad (2009b). 'Lifting events in RDF from interactions with annotated Web pages'. In: *The Semantic Web - ISWC 2009*. Vol. 5823. Lecture Notes in Computer Science. Springer Berlin / Heidelberg, pp. 893–908. ISBN: 978-3-642-04929-3. DOI: {10.1007/978-3-642-04930-9_56}.

Stühmer, Roland; Anicic, Darko; Sen, Sinan; Stojanovic, Nenad (2009c). 'Client-side Event Processing for Personalized Web Advertisement — [Demo]'. In: *Proceedings of the 3rd ACM International Conference on Distributed Event-Based Systems*. New York, NY, USA: ACM, pp. 1–2. ISBN: 978-1-60558-665-6. DOI: 10.1145/1619258.1619307.

Stühmer, Roland; Verginadis, Yiannis; Alshabani, Iyad; Morsellino, Thomas; Aversa, Antonio (2013). 'PLAY: Semantics-Based Event Marketplace'. In: *14th IFIP Working Conference on Virtual Enterprise – Special Session on Event-Driven Collaborative Networks*. Ed. by Luis M. Camarinha-Matos; Raimar J. Scherer. Vol. 408. IFIP Advances in Information and Communication Technology. Springer, pp. 699–707. DOI: 10.1007/978-3-642-40543-3_73.

Truptil, Sebastien; Barthe, Anne-Marie; Benaben, Frederick; Stühmer, Roland (2012). 'Nuclear Crisis Use-Case Management in an event-driven Architecture'. In: *Business Process Management Workshops*. Ed. by Florian Daniel; Kamel Barkaoui; Schahram Dustdar. ISBN: 978-3-642-28107-5. DOI: 10.1007/978-3-642-28108-2_45.

Villata, Serena; Delaforge, Nicolas; Gandon, Fabien (2011). *S4AC Vocabulary Specification*. Online resource. http://ns.inria.fr/s4ac Last accessed 2014-05-02.

Völkel, Max (2006). 'RDFReactor – From Ontologies to Programatic Data Access'. In: *Proc. of the Jena User Conference 2006*. HP Bristol.

Wagner, Andreas; Anicic, Darko; Stühmer, Roland; Stojanovic, Nenad; Harth, Andreas; Studer, Rudi (2010). 'Linked Data and Complex Event Processing for the Smart Energy Grid'. In: *Proc. of Linked Data in the*

Future Internet at the Future Internet Assembly. Ed. by Sören Auer; Stefan Decker; Manfred Hauswirth. Vol. 700. CEUR Workshop Proceedings ISSN 1613-0073.

Weaver, Jesse; Tarjan, Paul (2012). 'Facebook Linked Data via the Graph API'. In: *Semantic Web Journal*. DOI: 10.3233/SW-2012-0078.

Weidlich, Matthias; Mendling, Jan; Gal, Avigdor (2013). 'Net-Based Analysis of Event Processing Networks – The Fast Flower Delivery Case'. In: *Application and Theory of Petri Nets and Concurrency*. Ed. by José-Manuel Colom; Jörg Desel. Vol. 7927. Lecture Notes in Computer Science. Springer Berlin Heidelberg, pp. 270–290. ISBN: 978-3-642-38696-1. DOI: 10.1007/978-3-642-38697-8_15.

Xing, Ying; Zdonik, Stan; Hwang, Jeong-Hyon (2005). 'Dynamic Load Distribution in the Borealis Stream Processor'. In: *ICDE '05: Proceedings of the 21st International Conference on Data Engineering*. Washington, DC, USA: IEEE Computer Society, pp. 791–802. ISBN: 0-7695-2285-8. DOI: 10.1109/ICDE.2005.53.

Zhang, Ying; Duc, PhamMinh; Corcho, Oscar; Calbimonte, Jean-Paul (2012). 'SRBench: A Streaming RDF/SPARQL Benchmark'. In: *The Semantic Web — ISWC 2012*. Vol. 7649. Lecture Notes in Computer Science. Springer Berlin Heidelberg, pp. 641–657. ISBN: 978-3-642-35175-4. DOI: 10.1007/978-3-642-35176-1_40.

Index